A STRAIGHTFORWARD GUIDE
TO
BUYING AND SELLING
YOUR OWN HOME

Frances James

Straightforward Publishing

D0413317

British cataloguing in Publication Data. A Catalogue record of this publication is available in the British Library.

ISBN:

978-1-84716-751-4

4edge www.4edge.co.uk

Cover design by Bookworks Islington

CONTENTS

Introduction

SECTION 1 BUYING AND SELLING A HOME

3

INTRODUCTION

As time goes by, we either find ourselves in the middle of a housing market 'boom' or a 'bust'. Currently, at the time of writing, **2017**, we are experiencing an erratic cycle in house prices, the London market is continually growing due, it is said, to a lack of new housing. Whatever the cause, home ownership is beyond the reach of many in the South East generally. Other areas are also showing signs of growth..

However, notwithstanding market conditions, the process of buying and selling a home remains probably the single most important activity undertaken by individuals in their lifetime. The money and effort involved means that it is a process that must be carried out effectively and with a clear knowledge of the elements involved.

There are different people out there buying property, some private individuals and other buy-to-let investors. This book is aimed generally at those who are trying to buy and sell a property, and also covers those who wish to rent out properties, usually as 'casual landlords' as the title suggests.

When buying or selling a home, particularly buying, you will liase with a whole number of people, professional or otherwise: solicitors, estate agents, finance brokers, surveyors, banks and building societies and so on. All of these people play a vital role in the house purchase/sale transaction. All of these parties involved will have many years experience of property and not all of them will be acting in your own best interests.

Very often, the person who owns the property or who wishes to purchase a property is the one with the least knowledge of the process and is the one who stands to lose the most. When initially looking for a property, wrong decisions are made. The price paid for a property is quite often too high, with disastrous consequences later on. The condition of the property may leave a lot to be desired. There are many stories of people losing out on this single most important transaction. Unfortunately, it is a fact that if mistakes are made at the outset then you might spend the rest of your life recovering from the consequences.

Chapter 1

Buying a Home-Looking for a Home

Obviously, where you choose to buy your house will be your own decision. However, it may be your first time and you may be at a loss as to where to buy, i.e. rural areas or urban areas, the type and cost of property or whether a house or flat. There are several considerations here:

Area

Buying in a built up area has its advantages and disadvantages. There are normally more close communities, because of the sheer density. However, it is true to say that some built up areas have become fragmented by population movement, "Yuppification" etc. Local services are closer to hand and there is a greater variety of housing for sale. Transport links are also usually quite good and there are normally plenty of shops.

Disadvantages are less space, less privacy, more local activity, noise and pollution, less street parking, more expensive insurance and different schooling to rural environments. The incidence of crime and vandalism and levels of overall stress are higher in built up, more urban areas. This is not the case with all built up areas. It is up to the buyer to carry out research before making a commitment. If you are considering buying in a rural area, you might want to consider the following: there is more detached housing with land, more space and privacy. However, this can be undermined by the "village" syndrome where everyone knows your business, or wants to know your business. There is also cleaner air and insurance premiums can be lower. Disadvantages can be isolation, loneliness, lower level of services generally, and a limited choice of local education.

Choosing your property

You should think carefully when considering purchasing a larger property. You may encounter higher costs, which may include:

- Larger, more expensive, carpeting
- More furniture. It is highly unlikely that your existing furniture will suit a new larger home.
- Larger gardens to tend. Although this may have been one of the attractions, large gardens are time consuming, expensive and hard work.
- Bigger bills
- More decorating
- Higher overall maintenance costs

Valuing a property

In the main, buyers will leave it to estate agents to offer a fair price, or market price for the house. In a period of spiralling house price inflation which is now thankfully slowing down, although there was a re-occurrence of this in London, values were seemingly plucked out of the air. If you want to compare estate agents valuations with others then you can access one of the websites, such as www.hometrack or rightmove in order to gain a comparative value. Other sites are the Halifax, Nationwide, the Royal Institute of Chartered Surveyors, the National Association of Estate Agents and the Land Registry. You can also gain an idea of the valuation by looking in estate agents windows and assessing similar properties.

Purchasing a flat

There are some important points to remember when purchasing a flat. These are common points that are overlooked. If you purchase a flat in a block, the costs of maintenance of the flat will be your own. However, the costs of maintaining the common parts will be down to the landlord (usually) paid for by you through a service charge. There has been an awful lot of trouble with service charges, trouble between landlord and leaseholder. It has to be said that many landlords see service charges as a way of making profit over and above other income, such as ground rent, which is usually negligible after sale of a lease. However, having said that, the practice of developers fixing exorbitant ground rent rises into leases has been in the news at the time of writing (2017). The periodic doubling or trebling of ground rents has caused some leaseholders headaches when it comes to selling. Thankfully, most big house builders are taking steps to remedy this problem. The lesson is that if you purchase a leasehold property take a look at the ground rent provisions very carefully.

Many landlords will own the companies that carry out the work and retain the profit made by these companies. They will charge leaseholders excessively for works which are often not needed. The 1996 Housing Act (as amended by the Commonhold and Leasehold Reform Act 2002) attempts to strengthen the hand of leaseholders against unscrupulous landlords by making it very difficult indeed for landlords to take legal action for forfeiture (repossession) of a lease without first giving the leaseholder a chance to challenge the service charges.

Be very careful if you are considering buying a flat in a block – you should establish levels of service charges and look at accounts. Try to elicit information from other leaseholders. It could be that there is a leaseholders organisation, formed to manage their own service charges. This will give you direct control over contracts such as gardening, cleaning, maintenance contacts and cyclical decoration contracts. Better value for money is obtained in this way. In this case, at least you know that the levels will be fair, as no one leaseholder stands to profit. It is important to know that under the Leasehold Reform Act 1993 as amended by the Commonhold and Leasehold Reform Act 2002 all leaseholders have the right to extend the length of their lease by a term of 90 years. For example, if your lease has 80 years left to run you can extend it to 170 Years. There is a procedure in the above Act for valuation. Leaseholders can also collectively purchase the freehold of the block. There is a procedure for doing this in the Act although it is often time consuming and can be expensive. There are advantages however, particularly when leaseholders are not satisfied with management.

Viewing properties

Before you start house hunting, draw up a list of characteristics you will need from your new home, such as the number of bedrooms, size of kitchen, garage, study and garden. Take the estate agents details with you when viewing. Also, take a tape measure with you. Assess the location of the property. Look at all the aspects and the surroundings. Give some thought as to the impact this will have in your future life. Assess the building, check the facing aspect of the property, i.e., north, south etc. and check the exterior carefully. Earlier, I talked about the need to be very careful when assessing a property. When you have made your mind up, a survey is essential.

Look for a damp proof course - normally about 15cm from the ground. Look for damp inside and out. Items like leaking rainwater pipes should be noted, as they can be a cause of damp. Look carefully at the windows. Are they rotten? Do they need replacing and so on. Look for any cracks. These should most certainly be investigated. A crack can be symptomatic of something worse or it can merely be surface. If you are not in a position to make this judgement then others should make it for you.

Heating is important. If the house or flat has central heating you will need to know when it was last tested. Gas central heating should be tested at least once a year. Likewise, be very careful if the house or flat has electric storage heaters, particularly the older type as they can be very expensive to run.

You should look carefully at the EPC (Energy Performance Certificate) which the estate agent will usually have and which can be accessed online. This will give you an indication of the overall energy efficiency of the property and also what it might cost you to run.

All in all you need to remember that you cannot see everything in a house, particularly on the first visit. A great deal may be being concealed from you. In addition, your own knowledge of property may be slim. A second opinion is a must.

Buying an old house

If you are considering purchasing an older house and making improvements then there are a number of things to think about:

consider whether your proposed alterations will be in keeping with the age and style of the house, and neighbouring houses, particularly in a terrace. A classic mistake is that of replacing doors and windows with unsympathetic modern products. Again, salesmen will sell you anything and quite often won't provide the correct advice. If appropriate, you should consider contacting the Victorian Society vcitoriansociety.org or the Georgian Group georgiangroup.org.uk for advice on preserving your home. Both offer leaflets to help you carry out appropriate restoration. It is often a good idea to employ an architect or surveyor to oversee any alterations you are considering. For local contractors contact the Royal Institute of British Architects or Royal Institute of Chartered Surveyors.

Renovation grants

These may be available from local authorities, although there are stringent requirements. They are means tested and the higher your income the more you are expected to pay. For further details you should contact your local authority direct.

Disabled facilities grant

A grant may be available to adapt a property for a disabled person, for example improving access into and around the home and adapting existing facilities within it. These grants are mandatory, but a discretionary grant is available to make a property suitable for the accommodation, welfare or employment of a disabled person.

A leaflet, entitled Help for Disabled People with Adaptation and Other works, which can be obtained from your local authority, provides basic information.

Equalities Act 2010

The Equalites Act 2010, with effect from October 2010, has introduced an obligation on all landlords to ensure that, if a disabled person requests it, suitable disabled access to common parts, and within common parts is available. Again, information is available from the local authority.

Planning permission

If you are considering alterations of a significant nature, either internal or external, you may need planning permission from your local authority. You may need planning permission if you plan to change the look or external aspect of the building or if you are intending to change the use. You are allowed to carry out some work without planning permission, so it is worth contacting the local authority. You should also ask about building regulations. These are concerned with the materials and methods of building adopted. Regulations for work carried out in conservation areas are strict. The building control department at your local authority will be able to advise you about building regulations.

Buying a listed building

Buildings of architectural or historical interest are listed by the Secretary of State for National Heritage following consultation with English Heritage, to protect them against inappropriate alteration. In Wales, buildings are listed by the Secretary of State for Wales in consultation with CADW (Heritage Wales). In Scotland, they are listed by the Secretary of State for Scotland, in consultation with Historic Scotland. If you intend to carry out work to a listed building, you are likely to need listed building consent for any internal or external work, in addition to planning permission. The conservation officer in the local planning department can provide further information.

Buildings in conservation areas

Local authorities can designate areas of special architectural or historical significance. Conservation areas are protected to ensure that their character or interest is retained. Whole towns or villages may be conservation areas or simply one particular street. Strict regulations are laid down for conservation areas. Protection includes all buildings and all types of trees that are larger than 7cm across at 1.5m above the ground. There may be limitations for putting up signs, outbuilding or items such as satellite dishes. Any developments in the area usually have to meet strict criteria, such as the use of traditional or local materials. This also applies to property in national

19

parks, designated Areas of Outstanding Natural Beauty and the Norfolk or Suffolk Broads. Whether or not a property is listed or is deemed to be in a conservation area will show up when your conveyancer carries out the local authority search.

Buying a new house
Top tips for buying a new build home

New build homes are a great option whether you're a first time buyer, have a growing family or "right sizing" in later years. But there are also common problems many home buyers aren't aware of. There are benefits to buying a new home:

- Many people like the fact that they will be the first to live in the property
- Repairs and redecoration costs should be minimal for the first few years
- Buyers can often select fixtures and fittings to tailor the property finish to their taste
- New properties usually come with guarantees. As well as NHBC's 10-year warranty, other companies provide warranties and insurance for new homes, such as BLP's housing warranty insurance (blpinsurance.com).
- If the property is built to the correct standard, homeowners can enjoy lower running costs and energy bills

However, there can be problems, one of the main ones being the developer. Some are less than helpful. It is a fact that developers don't compete on quality and after sales service. the following might be helpful:

- Get to know the developers in the area where you want to buy and research them online. Look out for where they are mentioned on forums and see what people are saying. Don't let it put you off completely but let these forums inform you of the issues you need to be alive to.
- If the development has been partially completed ask the neighbours how they found the process of buying. You might pick up some top tips for negotiating and things to watch for in your contract.
- Visit the developer's other sites: How do they look? Do the new residents speak highly of their homes and the developer?
- Never rely solely on the developer's promotional material. Get a feel for what you're buying by visiting the site and the local area. Look at transport links, do your journey to work, walk to local facilities and so on.

The Home Owners Alliance hoa.org.uk is a very useful organisation to approach and provides many useful tips when buying a new home.

Pricing

A new build house will depreciate in price the minute you turn the key in the door. Even in a rising property market you may not get your money back if you have to sell within a year or two. There are ways to overcome this:

- Compare the new build home you are looking at with similar "old" properties in terms of value, space and rental value in the local area. Check the price per square foot, and compare it with the resale market so you understand the extent of the premium you will be paying.

- Negotiate with the developers. Find out what other properties on the site have been sold for on Zoopla or Rightmove. There can often be deals to be done at the end of their financial year, or when there are only a few properties left to be sold.

- Shop around for good deals. Many developers offer incentives to differentiate them from other local developers, such as free furnishings, a car parking space, or by paying your legal fees or stamp duty. If you can't negotiate money off the price, the offer to pay your stamp duty is probably the best freebie to take up as it will probably save you the most money, but be aware that any incentives offered by the developer over about 5% will impact on how much your lender is willing to hand out.

- Plan to stay put for a few years. Future proof your purchase by ensuring it fits with your personal plans for the next few years. Could your new partner move in? Could you comfortably fit a new baby in?

- Think about adding value. When buying think about whether there is scope to add value in the future – a conservatory on the back, or a landscaped garden or loft conversion. You may not be able to afford it now, but it may be an option in the future or make your home an attractive proposition to future buyers wanting to add value

Delays in moving in

This is particularly the case if you are buying "off plan" before the development has been completed. The Home Owners Alliance recommends that you get the builder to agree a 'long stop' completion date which means he'll be liable to pay you compensation if he doesn't finish the work by that date. The same organisation provides good advice on getting a mortgage for a new build property.

Workmanship and Finish

NHBC (National House Building Council) warranties and the like are not going to cover workmanship and quality finishes. So make sure you're happy at every stage of the build with how your new home is shaping up but especially before you complete. By the time you instruct solicitors you should have seen copies of the plans and specification of what the developer intends to build. The more detail this shows, the better.

Warranties

NHBC and similar guarantees are supposed to give peace of mind for the first 10 years after construction of the property. The policy attaches to the property, so that it benefits successive owners during the 10 year period. You should be aware however that the NHBC is an insurer and the guarantees are in reality insurance policies. If you make a claim, NHBC may use the small print to avoid paying for or carrying out remedial work.

Make sure there is a "snagging" provision in your contract to allow you to get little issues sorted – such as doors catching on carpets – directly with the developer. During the first two years from completion of your home, NHBC will step in if you make a claim against the developer *and* the developer fails to carry out the remedial work.

You should diarise the two year time limit, because if you want to make a claim under the initial guarantee you must notify the developer (in writing and copied to NHBC) before it expires. Even though the claim is made to the developer, NHBC have a dispute resolution service which you can use free of charge.

When it comes to your white goods – such as cookers, dishwashers, fridge freezers, hobs and washing machines and dryers – you have specified in your new home, you should ask the developer to hand over guarantees to you on completion. You'll want to have this stipulated in the contract.

A word about space standards

Research carried out recently shows that new-build houses have shrunk in size over the years, and compares today's homes with Victorian property. The main and obvious reason is the demand for land and the need to build more units on smaller plots of land.

The most drastically reduced properties are semi-detached homes which are down 33% from an average Victorian size of 1,662 sq ft to 1,100 sq ft today. Detached houses have shrunk by 30% and terraces by 13%. Reduced size means that you will have to work harder to get the best out of your property. This impacts on the size and nature of the furniture that you should use and also how you utilise the space you have.

Websites for housebuilders

Most developers have their own websites with details and picture of their developments. These include both new properties and refurbished. In addition there are several websites that specialise in new properties only. One such site is www.newhomesforsale.co.uk

Buying a Rented House-Right to Buy

If you rent your house from your council, you will be able to buy it at a discount under Right to Buy legislation. the current government has increased discounts in an attempt to increase the right to buy. If you live in a new town, a housing association or housing association trust, you would need to make enquiries, as many are exempt, although the government announced that it was introducing legislation to force Housing Associations to sell properties under the right to buy. A compromise has been reached where this will be voluntary. The following rules apply to the Right to Buy:

- You get a 35% discount if you've been a public sector tenant for between 3 and 5 years.
- After 5 years, the discount goes up by 1% for every extra year you've been a public sector tenant, up to a maximum of 70% – or £78,600 across England and £104,900 in London boroughs (whichever is lower).

Flats

- You get a 50% discount if you've been a public sector tenant for between 3 and 5 years.
- After 5 years, the discount goes up by 2% for every extra year you've been a public sector tenant, up to a maximum of 70% – or £78,600 across England and £104,900 in London boroughs (whichever is lower).

If your landlord has spent money on your home

Your discount will be less if your landlord has spent money building or maintaining your home:

- in the last 10 years - if your landlord built or acquired your home before 2 April 2012
- in the last 15 years - if you're buying your home through Preserved Right to Buy, or if your landlord acquired your home after 2 April 2012

You won't get any discount if your landlord has spent more money than your home is now worth.

Social Homebuy

With Social HomeBuy, you buy a share of your council or housing association home and pay rent on the rest of it. To apply, ask your landlord for an application form.

Discounts

You'll get a discount of between £9,000 and £16,000 on the value of your home, depending on:

- where your home is
- the size of the share you're buying

If you want to buy another share in your home later on, you'll get a discount on that too.

Buying more of your home later

You must buy at least 25% of your home. You can buy more later, until you own 100%. This is called 'staircasing'.

If you buy more of your home, your rent will go down - because it's based on how much of the property you rent. Your landlord can charge rent of up to 3% of the value of their share of your home, per year.

ExampleYour home is worth £240,000 and you buy a 50% share. Your landlord charges you 3% rent on their 50% share. 3% of £120,000 is £3,600 per year. This works out at £300 per month for you to pay in rent.

Who can't apply

You can't use Social HomeBuy if:

- you have an assured shorthold tenancy
- you're being made bankrupt
- a court has ordered you to leave your home
- your landlord is taking action against you for rent arrears, anti-social behaviour or for breaking your tenancy agreement

Not all local councils or housing associations have joined the scheme. Check with your landlord to find out if they belong to the scheme and whether your home is included

Help to Buy Schemes

See chapter 4 for more details on Help to Buy and how it might benefit you.

Shared/part ownership property

There are properties available on a shared/part ownership basis, usually from housing associations. Local Authorities also provide such schemes, although rarely. The main principle is that you buy a percentage of the property, say 50% and you rent the rest, with a service charge if a flat. As time goes by you can "staircase up" to 100% ownership. This is a scheme specially designed for those who cannot meet the full cost of outright purchase in the first instance. Usually, your total monthly outgoings are smaller than they would be if you purchased outright. Social Housing providers run a range of different schemes each year, largely depending on Government requirements. For further details you should contact a large housing association in your area who will provide you with current schemes on offer and point you in the right direction.

Self-build property

Self-build is another option for obtaining a new home. However, it is time consuming and not for the faint hearted. You need to be organised and to have organised the finances and your work programme. Usually the biggest problem is finding a suitable plot of land. There is a lot of competition. It also means that you will, unless you employ an agent, be charged with supervising a number of skilled craftsmen. Self-build usually works out cheaper than buying off a developer but it is certainly not an easy option. For more information and advice check out the following websites:

www.homebuilding.co.uk

This is run by the publishers of homebuilding and renovation magazine which is the leading magazine for homebuilders. The site is magazine style with lots of articles and also a link to www.plotfinder.net. This is a recently established database of land for sale and houses to renovate. There is an annual subscription cost, currently £48.60 (as at 2017/2018)

www.buildstore.co.uk

This site is owned by a group of venture capitalists, individuals and companies involved in the self build market. Again, there is a mix of articles and also adverts.

www.ebuild.co.uk

This site is published by specialist publisher's webguides on line. The site includes a directory of suppliers from architectural salvage to waste disposal with links to useful sites.

www.npbs.co.uk

This is the site of Norwich and Peterborough Building Society, who offer mortgages for self build projects. The loan for self-build is released in stages linked to the building of the property. It is worth checking to see if these mortgages are on offer. Other useful sites for self-build advice are:

www.self-build.co.uk

This site provides wide ranging self-build and renovation advice.

www.selfbuildportal.org.uk

The Self Build Portal is a Government-endorsed website for the would-be self builder - providing impartial advice and useful information on building your home.

There is a wealth of information about self build and how to go about it. Suffice to say that you need to be committed if you intend to go down this route. One of the best ways to glean information is to attend one of the many self-build forums around the country and learn from thos ewith experience in the area. The self-build-guide.co.uk is a good place to start as it provides links to various forums.

**

Chapter 2

The Role of Estate Agents in Buying and Selling Property

_____

Estate Agents

Estate agents are the normal route to buying or selling a home, although, as we will see later, online agents are prospering, offering cheaper deals for the sale or purchase of a property, many doing it for a fixed fee. However, a lot of people like the 'personal touch' and use agents. There are things to watch out for, particularly in London, where there is a big demand and short supply. Estate agents will often try to charge various 'fees' for services and tie people into different charges in the contract. Always demand to know the fees and be sure where you are before you enter into a contract.

What to expect from an estate agent:

- Advice on the selling or asking price of a house or flat - they know the local market
- Advice on the best way to sell (or buy) and where to advertise; they should discuss an advertising budget with you
- If selling, a meeting to visit, assess and value your home and

also to take down the particulars of your home. The Property Misdescriptions Act 2010, which arose out of the bad old days of the 1980's, prevents agents from using ambiguous statements to enhance the sale of the property. You should look at the points carefully as people who are disappointed after reading such a glowing report will not purchase.

- They may ask for details of recent bills, such as council tax and electricity. They should also be willing to give advice on fixtures and fittings included in the sale.

- They should be willing to show potential buyers around your home if you are not available.

- Don't expect to have to pay for a for-sale board although some lenders will try to make a charge.

Although a seller does not have any specific duty to disclose information about a property, estate agents have specific legal obligations not to mislead members of the public. Since 2013 agents have been covered by the general duties owed by other businesses to consumers that are set out in the Consumer Protection from Unfair Trading Regulations 2008.

These regulations include a ban on misleading statements or omissions and they effectively require estate agents to reveal any material facts about a property to potential buyers.

Choosing an agent if selling

Consider the following points:

- They ought to sell your type of property or specialise in one particular area of the market

- They should be a member of one of the professional bodies such as the National Association of Estate Agents, the Royal Institution of Chartered Surveyors, The Incorporated Society of Valuers and Auctioneers, The Architects and Surveyors Institute or the Association of Building Engineers.. Obtain quotes of fees, including the basic charge and any extras you might have to pay for, such as advertising in specialist publications.

Choose at least two agents to value the house, if instructing an agent. One more interesting point to note. One innovation that has appeared recently is that anyone, an average person, can be paid to show someone around a property. The app Viewber allows people to sign up as a stand-in for overstretched estate agents to conduct viewings on their behalf at anti-social times such as evenings and weekends. You might get an average of £20 per viewing, and they generally last less than half an hour. To sign up go to viewber.co.uk which will provide more details.

Sole agency selling.

Offering an agent sole agency may reduce the fee. This can be done for a limited time. After this you can instruct multiple agents. With sole agency you can sell privately, although you may still be liable for the sole agent's fee.

Joint sole agents

With this arrangement, two or more agents co-operate in the house sale and split the commission. The agents may charge a higher commission in this case.

Multiple agency

This means that you have several agents trying to sell your home, but only pay the agent who sells your property.

Agents agreements

You need to be careful when you use agents as if you decide to terminate the contract with one and move to another you need to be aware of the terms in the agency agreement you have signed. Estate agents commission is or should be spelt out in the agreement you sign. However, estate agents are also governed by the Estate Agents Act 1979, the Estate Agents (Provision of Information) Regulations 1991 and consumer protection legislation.

In essence, an agent must explain their commission arrangements to their clients in detail and draw their specific attention to any unusual or particularly onerous commission arrangements in the agency agreement. The usual requirement, as explained by Lord Neuberger in the 2008 case of Foxtons v Pelkey Bicknell is that the agent must be the 'effective cause' of the sale to receive a commission.

Buying property using the internet

There are a number of websites that also detail properties, some are independent and some are owned by the large players.

The following are a selection of the main sites:

www.rightmove.co.uk.

This is one of the largest sites, jointly owned and run by Halifax, Royal Sun Alliance, Connell and Countryside assured Group. They jointly claim to represent more than 170,000 properties covering 99% of UK postcodes.

The main function of this site is as a property search site, enabling people to search for property by name of area and postcode.

Each property has a reference number and will have a photo and details. These can be obtained by clicking on the property.

There is much useful information, including room sizes.

www.zoopla.co.uk

The claims of this website are that it can help the buyer to find a property, move home and settle in.

www.primelocation.co.uk

This site was launched in 2000 by a consortium of estate agents. This site deals with more expensive properties.

www.purplebricks.com

This is a very well known site and there are more and more of their boards on display. The differe3nce here is that purple bricks is an online estate agent and charges a lower fixed fee than the average estate agent. However, beware as despite the claims and testimonials on their blogs, you will get a lower level of service than a traditional estate agent. Traditional agents may charge more but you get more for your money, such as personal contact, viewings etc.

There are many more online agents springing up but think carefully before deciding to use them and weigh up the advantages and disadvantages.

Selling property using the internet

Although estate agents are still the main avenues for selling property, as we have seen, the web now plays a more significant part. In addition to the websites detailed, almost all agents now have their own website. This is really an electronic shop window where your property is displayed. Buyers interested in your property should be able to e-mail the estate agent directly for a viewing.

Ten top tips when selling a property

If you are selling a property, there are a number of things that you need to get right in order to ensure the best chance on the market:

- Get the price right-this is absolutely crucial-if you try to overprice then you will harm your chances of a sale as you will lose the trust of would-be purchasers-pitch the price attractively.
- Make your property presentable-remember that you are selling your home and you should show it to its best advantage.
- get the photos right
- make sure it is described fully-do not mss anything out.
- make your agent work for you. the first 30 days on the property market are crucial. make sure you are in regular contact with them. Don't forget to include a floor plan.
- make sure you have all the relevant certificates and paperwork, such as gas and electricity certificates, and damp proofing etc.

This advice applies whether you are using a traditional high street agent or are using an online agent. make sure that what you are selling is shown in its best light.

Chapter 3

Buying a Property-The Practicalities

Considerations when buying a house or flat

Budgeting

Before beginning to look for a house you need to sit down and give careful thought to the costs involved in the whole process. The starting point is to identify the different elements in the overall transaction.

Deposits

Sometimes the estate agent will ask you for a small deposit when you make the offer (see Estate Agents, chapter 2). This indicates that you are serious about the offer and is a widespread and legitimate practice, as long as the deposit is not too much, £100 is usual. The main deposit for the property, i.e., the difference between the mortgage and what has been accepted for the property, isn't paid until the exchange of contracts. Once you have exchanged contracts on a property the purchase is legally binding. Until then, you are free to withdraw. The deposit cannot be reclaimed after exchange.

Until the onset of the recession in 2009, banks would normally lend up to 95% of the purchase price of the property. However, particularly now, even though a few banks are willing to lend up to 95% the less you borrow the more favourable terms you can normally get from bank or building society. It has to be said that in the period leading up to the 'credit crunch' we were in a situation where banks loaned money to all and sundry at up to 125% of the value of the home plus exaggerated income multiples. Banks have now tightened up their lending criteria considerably. Recently, The Mortgage Market review came into effect (2014) which has imposed further restrictions on banks and building society lending and requires a stringent set of checks carried out before a mortgage is approved. many lenders like to see larger minimum deposits. This will vary with the bank or building society and you should also scan the Sunday newspapers in particular for details of best buys for mortgages. Refer to the previous chapter for details on the various schemes available, with the government providing help.

Stamp duty- What is stamp duty and who pays it?

Stamp Duty — Stamp Duty Land Tax (SDLT) official jargon — is a tax you pay when you buy a home. The buyer pays stamp duty – not the person selling. Stamp duty applies to both freehold and leasehold purchases over £125,000

2. How much do I have to pay?

Stamp duty used to be charged on the whole property price, so that it went up in big jumps. For example, if you bought a property for £250,000 you would have paid £2500 stamp duty; but if you bought a house costing just £1 more, you would tip into the next stamp duty bracket (what used to be 3%) and pay £7500 – a £5000 jump. This slab structure is gone now and from December 4, 2014 stamp duty is applied like income tax.

From April 2016, there has been a hike in stamp duty for buy to let properties (an extra 3% on top of the normal stamp duty and also on second homes. Stop press: From November 2017, first time buyers will be exempt from stamp duty on properties up to £300,000. Stamp duty is charged according to the scale below.

Purchase price of property	Stamp duty rate
Up to £125,000	Zero
Over £125,000 to £250,000	2%
Over £250,000 to £925,000	5%
Over £925,000 to £1.5 million	10%
Over £1.5 million	12%
Buy to let and second homes from 2016	3% surcharge

So, for example, for a residential property, if the agreed purchase price is £275,000, under the new rules, stamp duty is calculated:

0% on the first £125,000 = £0

2% on the next £125,000 = £2,500

5% on the final £ 25,000 = £1,250

Total stamp duty payable = £3,750

Special rates

There are different SDLT rules and rate calculations for:

- corporate bodies
- people buying 6 or more residential properties in one transaction
- shared ownership properties
- multiple purchases or transfers between the same buyer and seller ('linked purchases')
- purchases that mean you own more than one property
- companies and trusts buying residential property

Tax for properties held offshore

HMRC announced in March 2013, that an annual levy will now be made on properties held in British and Offshore companies, costing £2million or more. This is a measure to tackle tax avoidance. Those homes valued at between £2m-£5m will have to pay £15,000 per year; those between £5m-£10m will be taxed at £35,000; those with values of between £10m-£20m will pay £70,000 per year. owners of homes above £20m per year will have to pay £140,000 per year.

Whilst this is not likely to affect readers of this book, it is always better to be aware of such changes.

Other costs

A solicitor normally carries out conveyancing of property. However, individuals can do their own conveyancing, although it isn't as simple as it appears. All the necessary paperwork can be obtained from legal stationers and it is executed on a step-by-step basis. It has to be said that solicitors are now very competitive with their charges and, for the sake of between £600-£900, it is better to let someone else do the work which allows you to concentrate on other things. Another issue will be that your lender will not look favourably on you doing your own conveyancing and will usually insist on the use of a solicitor or licensed conveyancer..

Land Registry

The Land Registry records all purchases of land in England and Wales and is open to the public (inspection of records, called a property search). The registered title to any particular piece of land or property will carry with it a description and include the name of owner, mortgage, rights over other persons land and any other rights. There is a small charge for inspection. A lot of solicitors have direct links and can carry out searches very quickly. Not all properties are registered although it is now a duty to register all transactions.

(See chapter 6, conveyancing)

Energy Performance Certificates (EPC's)

EPC's are compulsory and are usually supplied by estate agents in their packs. An EPC surveyor will assess the property and looks at all the ways a house or flat can waste heat, such as inadequate loft insulation, lack of cavity wall insulation, draughts and obsolete boilers. After the assessment they will award a rating from A (as good as it gets) to G (terrible). The document also includes information and advice on how to improve matters, such as lagging the water tank or installing double-glazing. An EPC will cost between £120-130 and will be valid for ten years. Improvements made while the certificate is in force will not need a new survey.

Structural surveys

The basic structural survey is the homebuyers survey and valuation which is normally carried out by the building society or other lender. This will cost you between £250-£500 and is not really an in-depth survey, merely allowing the lender to see whether they should lend or not, and how much they should lend. Sometimes, lenders keep what they refer to as a retention, which means that they will not forward the full value (less deposit) until certain defined works have been carried out. If you want to go further than a homebuyers report then you will have to instruct a firm of surveyors who have several survey types, depending on how far you want to go and how much you want to spend.

A word of caution. Many people go rushing headlong into buying a flat or house. They are usually exhilarated and wish to complete their purchase fairly quickly in order to establish their new home. If you stop and think about this, it is complete folly and can prove very expensive later. A house or flat is a commodity, like other commodities, except that it is usually a lot more expensive. A lot can be wrong with the commodity that you have purchased which is not immediately obvious. Only after you have completed the deal and paid over the odds for your purchase do you begin to regret what you have done. The true price of a property is not what the estate agent is asking, certainly not what the seller is asking. The true market price is the difference between what a property in good condition is being sold at and your property minus cost of works to bring it up to that value.

Therefore, if you have any doubts whatsoever, and if you can afford it get a detailed survey of the property you are proposing to buy and get the works required costed out. When negotiating, this survey is an essential tool in order to arrive at an accurate and fair price. Do not rest faith in others, particularly when you alone stand to lose.

One further word of caution. As stated, a lot of problems with property cannot be seen. A structural survey will highlight those. In some cases it may not be wise to proceed at all.

Mortgage fees

Mortgage indemnity insurance. This is a one-off payment if you are arranging a mortgage over 70-80% of lenders valuation. This represents insurance taken out by the lender in case the purchaser defaults on payments, in which case the lender will sell the property to reclaim the loan. It is to protect the mortgage lender not the buyer. The cost of the insurance varies depending on how much you borrow. A 90% mortgage on a £60,000 property will cost between £300-600. For a 100% mortgage it is usually much higher. You have to ask yourself, if you are paying up to £2,000 for this kind of insurance on a 100% mortgage, is it not better to try to raise the money to put down a bigger deposit. Always think about the relative economics. A lot of money is made by a lot of people in house buying and selling. The loser is usually the buyer or seller, not the host of middlemen. So think carefully about what you are doing.

Mortgage arrangement fees

Depending upon the type of mortgage you are considering you may have to pay an arrangement fee. You should budget for a minimum of £400.

Buildings insurance

When you have purchased your property you will need to take out buildings insurance. This covers the cost of rebuilding your home if it is damaged. It also covers the cost of subsidence, storm and flood damage, burst pipes and other water leaks and vandalism and third party damage generally. The insurance company will tell you more about elements covered. It is worth shopping around for buildings insurance as prices vary significantly.

Many banks/building societies also supply buildings insurance if you arrange a mortgage with them. You shouldn't immediately take up their offer, as they are not always the most competitive. Websites such as www.confused.com can provide a range of quotes for you.

Removals

Unless you are not moving far and are considering doing it yourself, you should budget for hiring a removal firm. This will depend on how many possessions you have and how much time and money you have. Take care when choosing the removal firm. Choose one who comes recommended if possible.

There are other costs too. Reconnection of telephone lines and possibly a deposit, carpets, curtains and plumbing-in washing machines. How much you pay will probably depend on how handy you are yourself. There are also smaller incidental costs such as redirecting mail by the post office.

We will be discussing moving home in more depth later on in chapter 8.

Costs of moving

The table below will give you an idea of typical costs, such as solicitors fees, stamp duty, land registry fees and search fees when buying a property. The costs are based on a purchase of a typical London property. Other costs as discussed above will be extra. It has to be stressed that, apart from the stamp duty and Land Registry Fees solicitor's costs and searches will vary. Searches will cost more in different areas and solicitors fees will come down. (remember, stamp duty abolished up to £300,000 for first time buyers.)

House price	Solicitors fees (av)	Stamp duty	Land Registry	Search fees	Total fees
£150,000	£900	£500	200	200	1800
£200,000	£900	£1500	200	200	£2800
£300,000	£1000	5000	280	235	6,515
£500,000	£1000	15,000	280	280	16,560
£750,000	1069	27,500	280	280	29129
£1m	1372	66250	920	235	68777
£1.5m	1895	116,500	920	235	119550
£2m	2208	166,500	920	235	169863
£2.5m	2723	236500	920	235	240378
£3m	3656	260,000	920	235	264811
£3.5m	4231	310,000	920	235	315386
£4m	4871	360,000	920	235	366026

The process of buying a property

Having considered the basic elements of buying a property, the next step is to find the property you want. As we have discussed, this is a long and sometimes dispiriting process. Trudging around estate agents, sorting through mountains of literature, dealing with mountains of estate agents details, scouring the papers and walking the streets! However, most of us find the property we want at the end of the day. It is then that we can put in our offer. One useful way of determining the respective values of property in different areas is to visit a website set up for that purpose www.hometrack.co.uk. This particular site collects price information from selected estate agents in different postcode areas across the country. At the time of writing, prices are currently available for London and the southeast, the southwest, Birmingham and the Midlands and the north of England. Before you decide to look, a little research into prices and comparisons with what you can afford might be useful.

Making an offer

You should put your offer in to the estate agent or direct to the seller, depending who you are buying from. As discussed earlier, your offer should be based on sound judgement, on what the property is worth not on your desire to secure the property at any cost. A survey will help you to arrive at a schedule of works and cost. If you cannot afford to employ a surveyor from a high street firm then you should try to enlist other help. In addition, you should take a long and careful look at the house yourself, not just a cursory glance. Look at everything and try to get an idea of the likely cost to you of rectifying defects. However, I cannot stress enough the importance of getting a detailed survey. Eventually, you will be in a position to make an offer for the property. You should base this offer on sound judgement and you should provide a rationalisation for your offer, if it is considerably lower than the asking price. You should make it clear that your offer is subject to contract and survey (if you require further examination or wish to carry out a survey after the offer).

Putting your own home on the market

Most people moving try to secure the sale of their own home before looking for a new one. If you haven't started to sell your house yet, you are advised to do so as soon as possible. You need also to arrange finance. A lot of people have had the nightmarish experience of stepping into an estate agents and being besieged by "independent" financial advisors wishing to sell you their product. Be very careful at this stage. See "getting your mortgage" chapter 5.

Exchange of contracts

Once the buyer and seller are happy with all the details stated in the contract and your conveyancer can confirm that there are no outstanding legal queries, those conveyancing will exchange contracts. The sale is now legally binding for both parties. You should arrange the necessary insurances, buildings and contents from this moment on as you are now responsible for the property.

Buying with a friend

The 1996 Family Law Act brought in the concept of cohabiting couples having the same rights as married couples. This will apply particularly if your marriage starts to break up and you wish to ascertain property rights. However, it is wise to draw up a cohabitation contract prior to purchase which will put in writing how the property is shared and will make clear the situation after break-up. The cohabitation contract can include any conditions you wish and is drawn up usually by a solicitor. There are standard forms for cohabitation agreements which can include financial arrangements stating who pays for the mortgage, who can call for a sale, mutual wills, and who pays for and owns possessions. You can obtain a leaflet concerning this from a Citizens Advice Bureau or from a solicitor.

Completing a sale

This is the final day of the sale and normally takes place around ten days after Exchange. Exchange and completion can take place on the same day if necessary but this is unusual.

On day of completion, you are entitled to vacant possession and will receive the keys. See chapter 6 for more details on the conveyancing process.

Buying at auction

Although many people will go through the traditional route of acquiring property through an estate agent, there are other routes, one main one being the auction. Buying at auction requires a different set of skills and you need to know what you are buying, where it is and what the problems are, if any. Why is it being sold at auction? Certainly, you need to act fairly quickly as you need to inspect the property before auction day, arrive at the final bid price that you will not exceed and be prepared to complete within 28 days.

What is a property auction?

The process is very similar to the normal method of private sale. However, for an auction sale the seller and their solicitor carry out all the necessary paperwork and legal investigations prior to the auction. Subject to the property receiving an acceptable bid, the property will be 'sold' on auction day with a legally binding exchange of contracts and a fixed completion date.

Different types of property auction houses

Auction houses vary in size and the amount of business that they conduct and the frequency with which they hold auctions. Most will sell both residential and commercial property and each will have its own style of operation, and fee structure. Large auction houses will hold auctions frequently, perhaps every two months and will have around 250 lots for sale. A lot of the auctions happen in London. Most of the large auction houses will deal with property put forward by large institutions, such as banks selling repossessions.

Also local authorities and will advertise the sales in the mainstream media and trade papers. The medium size auction houses will hold auctions as frequently as they can, in regional venues, such as racecourses and conference centres, and depending on stock, usually every two to three months, tending to advertise locally. The small auction houses will have far fewer lots and will hold their sales in smaller local venues. They may advertise in local press but more often will trade on word of mouth.

Those who attend auctions

As you might imagine, all sorts of people attend auctions. The common denominator is that they are all interested in buying property.

Property investors are most common at auction, people who are starting out building a portfolio or those who have large portfolios that they wish to expand. They tend to fall into two groups, those who are after capital appreciation, i.e. buy at a low value and build the capital value and those who are looking for rental income. Then there are the property traders who like a quick profit from buying and 'flipping' property. These types usually have intimate knowledge of an area and are well placed to make a quick profit. Then we have the developers who look for small profitable sites or larger sites where property can be built and sold on. The sites can have existing buildings on them or can be vacant lots with or without planning permission. Last, but not least, we have those people who intend to buy solely for the purpose of owner occupation, look to buy a below-value property that they can redesign and make their own.

What types of property are suitable for auction?

There is strong demand for all types of properties offered at auction. These may be properties requiring updating, those with short leases, development sites with or without planning permission, repossessions, forced sales and, investment properties. Also ground rents, probates, receivership sales and local authority properties. However, any type of property can be sold at auction and initially the property will be inspected to discuss specific criteria and the current situation. Extensive research will be carried out by the auction house and advice offered as to whether auction is the appropriate method of sale. The below represents a cross section of what might be found at auction.

Properties for Improvement

Properties in need of updating make ideal auction Lots. They are in great demand from refurbishment specialists and private buyers, keen to undertake a project for their own occupation or for resale. They also appeal to buy-to-let investors who carry out the improvements then retain them as part of a property portfolio.

Tenanted Properties

Residential houses and flats with tenants in residence sell well at auction. Notice doesn't need to be served on tenants, and rental income continues to be received right up to completion.

Residential Investments

Houses in multiple occupation and blocks of flats are sold at auction as valuable investments. Here it is the rent level that determines the sale price, just as much as the building itself.

Development Propositions

Derelict or disused farm buildings, empty commercial premises, buildings with potential for conversion or change of use, can all sell well at auction. In some locations a change to residential can significantly add to the value of a property, in other situations there may be space for additional dwellings or to substantially enlarge the property.

Building Land

There is no better way of ensuring a seller achieves best price for a building plot or parcel of development land than to offer it for sale by auction. Builders will be able to consult with architects, planners etc., and be ready to bid in the auction room.

Mixed-Use Properties

Properties that have twin uses or a variety of potential future uses are ideal for sale by auction. Retail shops with accommodation above appeal to investors as well as owner-occupiers. Further conversion work can often be undertaken and the property tailored to suit the purchaser's special requirements.

Commercial Investments

Retail shops, offices, industrial units, garage blocks and parking areas - an ever increasing number of commercial investments are being sold at auction. It doesn't matter whether they are vacant or tenanted, with lease renewal soon needed or with a long way to run.

Unique Properties

There are always some rare entries, sought after property and prime locations that need to be sold in a competitive bidding environment. Unexpectedly high prices have been achieved by this route.

Amenity Land and Other Property

Paddocks, meadows, fields, moorings, amenity land and also other unusual land parcels are all sold at auction. If it is property or land that is surplus to requirements, the likelihood is a buyer can be found at auction.

Why is property being sold at an auction?

There are a number of reasons why property is sold at an auction:

- A quick sale is needed, often due to the owner being in financial difficulties or it is a repossession
- There are structural problems which prevent the property being sold easily in the conventional manner.
- Properties sold by public bodies. Here you get all sort of property, including weird and wonderful properties such as public toilets and police stations, all of which may have their uses.
- The property is unique and there are no direct comparisons, such as lighthouses and the above mentioned public toilet.

It is always best to find out why exactly the property is being sold at auction. Is it so difficult to get rid of because of some inherent reason? Ask why is this property at auction and not being sold in the conventional way? Who exactly is the vendor and what if any are the problems stopping it being sold conventionally? The reasons that the property is at auction may be entirely innocent but it is always worth finding out to avoid future problems.

What happens next?

Once you have found your auction, to receive a complimentary auction catalogue you should contact the Auctioneers and this will give the information about the properties being offered for sale. You can also download a catalogue from the auctioneers website. The catalogue includes descriptions of the available properties, legal information, viewing arrangements and a guide price, which is purely an indication of a realistic selling price. This should not be taken as a firm asking or selling price and should be relied upon as a guide only. Professional advice must be taken in relation to any lot in which there is an interest.

For lots where viewings are arranged, these are carried out on a block basis and are published in all advertising and in the auction catalogue.

Any prospective purchaser is welcome at these viewings and should the scheduled appointments be inconvenient, alternative arrangements can be made. Any interest must be registered with the Auctioneers in order that prospective purchasers may be kept informed as to the progress of the sale.

Bidding for a property

The lots will be offered and the bidding taken to the highest possible level and once the gavel falls, the contracts will be exchanged. The buyer purchases the property at the price they bid - this cannot be negotiated and the stipulated terms cannot be changed. The buyer will then pay 10% of the purchase price on the day and completion occur 28 days later. The funds are then paid to the seller less the fees of the Auctioneers and those of the seller's solicitor.

The atmosphere of an auction room can be extremely exciting and competitive and it is often the case that an interested party will bid in excess of the figure that had previously been set as their maximum. In some cases, the prices achieved at auction can be higher than those achieved by private treaty. The seller will provide a legal pack that may be inspected at any time. Auctioneers will strongly advise that professional advice is obtained from a legal representative. Details of the seller's solicitors will be available and, should a mortgage be required, it is advisable to have this in place prior to the sale. Again, Auctioneers strongly advise that funding is discussed with a professional advisor prior to attending the sale. The successful buyer will be required to pay 10% of the purchase price on the day, together with a buyer's premium which is normally £250 including VAT. The balance of the purchase price is required on the agreed completion day and this is normally 28 days after the auction, however this can vary so best to check with the auction house.

How do prospective purchasers find out legal and survey information for the properties in which they are interested?

A legal pack is requested from each of the vendor's solicitors and this contains copies of all legal papers, which will be required by any prospective purchasers for them to make an informed decision regarding the purchase of any lot. The pack will include office copy entries and plans, the relevant local authority search, leases (if applicable), Special Conditions of Sale, replies to pre-contract enquiries and any other relevant documents. A copy of these legal packs can usually be obtained from auctioneers for a small charge. Should any additional information be required, the seller's solicitors are listed in the catalogue and can be contacted directly. All legal packs are available for inspection at each auction.

Any purchase at auction takes place under the assumption that documentation and the terms of the contract have been read. It is strongly recommended that any potential purchasers carry out full investigations for any lot in which they have an interest and a survey is an integral part of that investigation.

How is finance arranged?

Should a mortgage be required, approval in principle must be obtained prior to auction. Lenders are now familiar with the auction process and are usually willing to provide a mortgage offer for buyers intending to purchase at auction. A valuation and survey will be required along with legal evidence that there are no issues that will affect the value.

It is essential that the lender can provide funds within the timescale for completion. On the day of the auction, the purchaser will need to pay 10% of the purchase price and must ensure there are cleared funds to pay this amount. Sometimes, finance can be arranged through an Auctioneers on request.

Can lots be bought before auction?

Vendors may consider offers submitted before auction day. Any such offers need to be submitted in writing to an Auctioneers - this will be referred to the vendor and their instruction will be passed on to the prospective purchaser. Any offers will have to be unconditional and the buyer must be in a position to exchange contracts and pay the required deposit before auction day. With most auctioneers, no offers are considered within five days of the auction.

What should I take with me to the auction room?

The items required are as follows:

- Deposit cheque or banker's draft for any potential purchase
- Identification - this is legally required under the money laundering regulations. Therefore a driving licence or passport is required and a current utility bill to show proof of residence.

- Details of solicitors acting on behalf of any potential purchaser.

What happens if a prospective purchaser is unable to attend the auction?

If prospective purchasers are unable to attend the sale, it is possible to bid in other ways:

- By telephone - the interested party will be telephoned as the lot is being auctioned.

- By proxy in writing - a member of the auction team will represent the buyer, who has previously specified their maximum bid

In each case a registration form and cheque to cover the deposit and buyer's fee, are required prior to the date of the auction. A bidder's registration form is printed in the catalogue or alternatively can be obtained from the office

Will the property be insured when I purchase?

No - the purchaser at auction is responsible for obtaining Building insurance cover from the moment the property is deemed sold to them at auction.

Sale by tender

As an alternative to auction, sale by tender is like a blind auction;

you don't know what the other potential buyers are offering. A form of tender is included in the sales details and sometimes sets out the contract details. Always check these details with your conveyancer, because often you cannot pull out after the offer is accepted.

Buyers put their offers in an envelope, sometimes with a 10% deposit. These must be received by the seller's agent at a specified date, at which time the seller will accept one of the offers.

Sale by tender is sometimes used when there have been two or three offers at similar prices.

House swapping

House swapping is an unorthodox but cost effective way of obtaining the property that you are looking for. It is a very efficient way of buying a property. Essentially, you find the property that you want and the seller moves into your house. There is no chain because you are cutting out other buyers. Obviously, the biggest problem is finding someone that you want to swap with and who wants to swap with you.

In practice, the estate agent should be the ideal key player in any swap arrangement. They have a large number of people on their books and who have provided details of their requirements. However, this way of operating seems to be beyond all but the most enterprising estate agencies. In practice, most swaps happen through coincidence.

Saving money through swapping homes

There is a significant saving to be made by swapping homes. If you are the one trading down, for example you have a home worth £275,000 and you want to swap it for a flat worth £150,000, the owner of the flat will be paying for your house with part cash part property. As far as HMRC is concerned this is not a sale on which you would pay stamp duty, but a transfer on which you would pay a notional sum of just £5. However, in this particular type of transaction solicitors must draw up the deal as a single contract with the more expensive property paid partly in kind and partly in cash. You can also save on estate agents fees if you find your swap independently. A useful website dealing with home swaps is:

www.home-swap.org.uk. Registration on the site is free.

Chapter 4

More About Mortgages

Most people purchasing a property will need a mortgage. There are many products on the market and deposits are not always required. However, it is crucial that you are in possession of all the facts when making a decision about a mortgage.

Financial advisers will give you plenty of advice but not always the best advice. Sometimes it is better to go to the lender direct. Before you talk to lenders, work out what your priorities are, such as tax advantage, early repayment and so on. Make sure that you are aware of the costs of life cover.

Lenders-Banks and building societies

There is little or no difference between the mortgages offered by banks and building societies. Because banks borrow against the wholesale money markets, the interest rate they charge to borrowers will fluctuate (unless fixed) as and when their base rate changes. Building societies however, which will rely more heavily on their savers deposits to fund their lending, may adjust the interest rate charged for variable mortgages only once a year. This may be a benefit or disadvantage, depending on whether rates are going up or down.

Centralised lenders

Centralised lenders borrow from the money markets to fund their lending and have no need for the branch network operated by banks and building societies. Centralised lenders, which came to the fore during the 1980s, particularly the house price boom, have been criticised for being quick to implement increases but slow to implement decreases, through rate reductions. This is, simply, because they exist to make profit. Therefore, you should be cautious indeed before embarking on a mortgage with lenders of this kind.

Brokers and "independent" financial advisors

Brokers act as intermediaries between potential borrowers and mortgage providers. If they are "tied" agents they can only advise on the products of one bank, insurance company or building society. If they are independent they should, technically, advise and recommend on every product in the market place. A word of warning. It is up to you to ask detailed questions about any product a broker offers you. Since 2013, advisors have to charge a fee and advertise this fee. Prior to this they charged a commission, the costs of which fell onto the borrower. Many brokers sell unsuitable products because they receive healthy commissions. In the 1980s it became impossible to enter an estate agents without being forced to enter into discussions with financial advisers who were intent on selling you products which made them a lot of money. If possible, you should arrange a mortgage direct with a bank and avoid so called independent brokers.

How much can you borrow?

There is a standard calculation for working out the maximum mortgage that you will be allowed. For one borrower, three times annual salary, for a joint mortgage, two or two and a half times combined. Lenders, however, will vary and some will lend more. Be very careful not to overstretch yourself. As stated, banks and building societies have tightened up their lending criteria and mortgages are hard to obtain without hefty deposits. The Financial Conduct Authority have introduced tough new rules to ensure that no one can borrow more than they can afford to repay. These rules represent a further tightening up after the fiasco of the last ten years which has ultimately led to the present crisis. Under the new rules, interest only mortgages will only be offered to people with a firm and clear repayment plan, rather than simply relying on the rise in house prices to cover repayment of the capital. Lenders will also have to take account of future interest rate increases on repayment costs.

Mortgage Market Review

New rules came into force in April 2014 means that those seeking a mortgage should brace themselves for a long wait to see a mortgage adviser, three-hour interviews at the bank and forensic analysis of your daily spending habits.

Even after jumping through all those hoops, success is not guaranteed – experts have warned thousands of buyers and home owners are likely to be rejected because they do not meet the new requirements.

The City regulator, the Financial Conduct Authority (FCA), has introduced the new rules, known as the Mortgage Market Review, to ensure borrowers are issued with mortgages they can afford both now and in the future. The FCA was concerned that lenders were making it too easy to get a mortgage before the financial crisis. Many households borrowed too much money and found they were unable to keep up their repayments when the financial crisis struck.

So-called "self-cert" loans, where borrowers declared their income but did not have to prove or "certify" it, were common and people routinely exaggerated earnings to borrow more. Interest-only loans also caused problems. Borrowers flocked to these deals because their monthly repayments were lower, but they had no way to repay the capital at the end of the loan.

To ensure safer lending in future, mortgage providers are now responsible for assessing whether customers can afford the loan in the long term. This includes buyers and those who are remortgaging and want to increase the size of the loan, vary the time frame or transfer it to a new property.

Deposits

Most banks and building societies used to lend 95% maximum, some more than that. It is now possible, if you look around, to get a high loan to valuation as there is a lot of competition with low interest rates here to stay for the moment, although as always, lenders will usually require higher deposits. The best source of information for reputable lenders is in the weekend newspapers. However, still, the more that you put down the better deal that you are likely to get from the lender.

Government Help-to-Buy Scheme

Help to Buy equity loan

You can get a low-interest loan towards your deposit. This is called an equity loan.

Eligibility

The home you buy must:

- be a new build
- have a purchase price of up to £600,000 in England (or £300,000 in Wales)
- be the only one you own
- not be sub-let or rented out after you buy it
- be one that you can show you can't afford (if you're applying in Wales)

How it works

With an equity loan:

- you need a 5% deposit
- the government will lend you up to 20% (up to 40% in London)
- you need a mortgage of up to 75% for the rest (up to 55% in London)

You must buy your home from a registered Help to Buy builder .There are different rules for equity loans in Wales.

Example

For a £200,000 property	Amount		Percentage	
Cash deposit	£10,000		5%	
Equity loan	£40,000	(£80,000 in London)	20%	(40% in London)
Mortgage	£150,000	(£110,000 in London)	75%	(55% in London)

Equity loan fees

You'll have to pay equity loan fees, but not for the first 5 years. In the sixth year, you'll be charged a fee of 1.75% of the loan's value.

The fee then increases every year, according to the Retail Prices Index plus 1%. Your Help to Buy agent will contact you to set up these monthly fee payments. You'll also get a statement about your loan each year. Fees don't count towards paying back the loan.

Paying back the loan

You must pay back the loan after 25 years or when you sell your home - whichever comes first. The amount you pay back depends on how much your home is worth (the market value).

Example

Market value of your home	Equity loan	Amount
Bought for £200,000	20%	Borrowed £40,000
Sold for £250,000	20%	Pay back £50,000

You can pay back part or all of your loan at any time. The smallest repayment you can make is 10% of the market value of your home.

Example

Market value of your home	Percentage	Amount
Bought for £200,000	Borrowed 20%	£40,000

Market value of your home   **Percentage**   **Amount**

Value at time of payment £220,000 Paying back 10% £22,000

How to apply

Apply through the:

- Help to Buy agent in the area where you want to live, for England
- housing association, for Wales

Help to Buy ISA

If you're saving to buy your first home, the government will top up your savings by 25% (up to £3,000). If you're buying with someone else, they can also get a Help to Buy ISA.

You don't have to pay it back.

Eligibility

The home you buy must:

- have a purchase price of up to £250,000 (or up to £450,000 in London)
- be the only home you own
- be where you intend to live

How it works

Your first payment to your ISA can be up to £1,200 and then you can pay up to £200 each month. When you buy your property, your solicitor or conveyancer will apply for the extra 25%.

Example

Your savings	Government payment	Total
£1,600 (minimum)	£400	£2,000
£4,000	£1,000	£5,000
£12,000 (maximum)	£3,000	£15,000

How to apply

Apply to one of the following providers:

- Aldermore Bank
- Bank of Scotland
- Barclays
- Clydesdale Bank
- Halifax
- HSBC
- Lloyds Bank
- Nationwide
- NatWest
- Newcastle Building Society

- Santander
- Ulster Bank
- Virgin Money
- Yorkshire Bank

Buying through shared ownership

You can get a shared ownership home through a housing association. You buy a share of your home (between 25% and 75%) and pay rent on the rest. There are different rules in Northern Ireland and Scotland. Contact your local authority to find out about buying a shared ownership home in Wales.

Eligibility

You can buy a home through shared ownership if your household earns £80,000 a year or less (or £90,000 a year or less in London) and any of the following apply:

- you're a first-time buyer
- you used to own a home, but can't afford to buy one now
- you're an existing shared owner

Older people

If you're aged 55 or over you can buy up to 75% of your home through the Older People's Shared Ownership (OPSO) scheme. Once you own 75% you won't pay rent on the rest.

Disabled people

You can apply for a scheme called home ownership for people with a long-term disability (HOLD) if other Help to Buy scheme properties don't meet your needs, eg you need a ground-floor property. With this scheme you can buy up to 25% of your home. If you're disabled you can also apply for the general shared ownership scheme and own up to 75% of your home.

Buying more shares

You can buy more of your home after you become the owner. This is known as 'staircasing'. The cost of your new share will depend on how much your home is worth when you want to buy the share. It will cost:

- more than your first share if property prices in your area have gone up
- less than your first share if property prices in your area have gone down

The housing association will get your property valued and let you know the cost of your new share. You'll have to pay the valuer's fee.

Selling your home

If you own a share of your home, the housing association has the right to buy it first. This is known as 'first refusal'. The housing association also has the right to find a buyer for your home. If you own 100% of your home, you can sell it yourself.

How to apply

To buy a home through a shared ownership scheme contact the Help to Buy agent in the area where you want to live.

Joint mortgages

If you want a joint mortgage, as for any other shared loan you and your partner have a shared responsibility for ensuring that the necessary repayments are made. If something happens to one partner then the other has total responsibility for the loan.

Main types of mortgage

Endowment

With this type of mortgage, you have to take out an endowment insurance policy which is then used to pay off the mortgage loan in a lump sum at the end of the term. There are a number of different types designed to achieve the same end:

- Low cost with profits. This is the usual sort of endowment, guaranteeing to pay back part of the loan only. However, because bonuses are likely to be added, it is usually enough to pay off the loan in full;

- Unit linked endowment. With this, the monthly premiums are used to buy units in investment funds. The drawback is that there is no guarantee how much the policy will be worth on maturity, since this depends on how well the investments have performed.

A word of warning. Endowment products were pushed heavily by financial brokers. There was an obsession with them in the 1980's. This is because they earn big commission for those people that sell them. Like a lot of salespeople, motivated by greed salespeople, some advisers failed to reveal the down side. This is:

-Endowments are investment linked and there is no guarantee that they will have matured sufficiently at the end of the term to repay the mortgage. This leaves you in a mess. A repayment mortgage will definitely have paid off the mortgage at the end of the term. If you change your mortgage and decide that you do not wish to continue with an endowment mortgage, and so cash in the policy early you will almost certainly get a poor return unless it is close to maturity. In the early years of the policy, most of your payments will go towards administration and commission (a fact that your broker does not always reveal). The alternative in these circumstances is to maintain the endowment until it matures, treating it as a stand-alone investment which will, hopefully, make you some money eventually.

Repayment mortgages

This mortgage, where the borrower makes regular repayments to pay the mortgage off over the term is a fairly safe bet. However, if you plan to move house every five years then this will not necessarily be the best mortgage for you. With a repayment mortgage, you pay interest every month but only a small proportion of the capital, particularly in the early years of the mortgage. An endowment mortgage, while more risky, could be better for you under these circumstances, since you can transfer the plan from property to property, while it can, hopefully, grow steadily as it matures.

Pension mortgages

A Pension mortgage is an interest only mortgage with an additional investment plan in the form of a personal pension. A personal pension is a stock market based investment that benefits from tax relief and tax free growth.

A pension pays a tax free lump sum and a monthly taxed income on retirement. The lump sum is normally used to pay off the mortgage.

Pros and Cons of Pension mortgages
Advantages
- Pension contributions benefit from up to 40% tax relief for higher rate tax payers.

Disadvantages

- Your mortgage debt remains constant throughout the mortgage period.

- You have no guarantee that you will have sufficient funds to pay off the mortgage at the end of the repayment period, as the pension fund could perform below expectations. (By monitoring your pension fund's performance, you could make additional contributions during the repayment period if you felt it was under performing.)

- The lump sum cannot be used for other purposes. You therefore need to ensure that your level of pension contributions are sufficient enough to maintain your required standard of living during retirement.

- The mortgage period may be longer than 25 years, depending on your age. You will still need to meet interest rate payments throughout this period.

Interest only mortgage

The borrower pays interest only on the loan, and decides how he or she will pay the loan off at the end. The lender will want to know this too, particularly in the light of the new rules being introduced, mentioned above.

Mixed mortgages

A new development is that one or two lenders now allow borrowers to mix a combination of mortgages in one deal, customising the mortgage to suit each individual.

Foreign currency mortgages

Some foreign banks offer short-term mortgages in the foreign currency of that bank. Their lending criteria can be much more relaxed than trying to borrow from a British lender. The advantage of this sort of mortgage depends on currency fluctuations. If the pound is stable or rises, the borrower benefits. If the pound drops, the borrower will have to pay more.

These types of home loans should be left to more sophisticated investors as there is the potential to get into trouble unless you have a clear grasp on the implications of such a mortgage.

Cashbacks

You probably saw the adverts offering large sums of cashback if you took a particular product. If you read the small print, unless you took the highest mortgage available with the highest deposit then you would not get anywhere near such a sum. This mortgage was typical of the many mortgages on offer in the pre-credit crunch times. You would be very hard pushed to see such an offer now.

Buy to Let Mortgages

Buy-to-let (BTL) mortgages are for landlords who buy property to rent it out. The rules around buy-to-let mortgages are similar to those around regular mortgages, but there are some key differences. Read on for more information about how they work, how to get one and what mistakes to avoid.

Who can get a buy-to-let mortgage?

You can get a buy-to-let mortgage if:

- You want to invest in houses or flats.
- You can afford to take a risk. Investing in property is risky, so you shouldn't take out a BTL mortgage if you can't afford to take that risk.
- You already own your own home. You'll struggle to get a buy-to-let mortgage if you don't already own your own home, whether outright or with an outstanding mortgage.
- You have a good credit record and aren't stretched too much on your other borrowings such as your existing mortgage and credit cards.
- You earn £25,000+ a year. Otherwise you might struggle to get a lender to approve your buy-to-let mortgage.
- You're under a certain age. Lenders have upper age limits, typically between 70 or 75. This is the oldest you can be when

the mortgage ends not when it starts. For example, if you are 45 when you take out a 25-year mortgage it will finish when you're 70.

How do buy-to-let mortgages work?

Buy-to-let mortgages are a lot like ordinary mortgages, but with some key differences:

- Interest rates on buy-to-let mortgages are usually higher.
- The fees also tend to be much higher.
- The minimum deposit for a buy-to-let mortgage is usually 25% of the property's value (although it can vary between 20-40%).
- Most BTL mortgages are interest-only. This means you don't pay anything each month, but at the end of the mortgage term you repay the capital in full.
- Most BTL mortgage lending is not regulated by the Financial Conduct Authority (FCA). There are exceptions, for example, if you wish to let the property to a close family member (e.g. spouse, civil partner, child, grandparent, parent or sibling). These are often referred to as a consumer buy to let mortgages and are assessed according to the same strict affordability rules as a residential mortgage.

How much you can you borrow for buy-to-let mortgages

The maximum you can borrow is linked to the amount of rental income you expect to receive. Lenders typically need the rental income to be a 25–30% higher than your mortgage payment. To find out what your rent might be talk to local letting agents, or check the local press and online to find out how much similar properties are rented for.

Where to get a buy-to-let mortgage

Most of the big banks and some specialist lenders offer BTL mortgages. It's a good idea to talk to a mortgage broker before you take out a buy-to-let mortgage, as they will help you choose the most suitable deal for you.

Using price comparison websites

Comparison websites are a good starting point for anyone trying to find a mortgage tailored to their needs. the following are the most popular.

- Moneyfacts
- Money Saving Expert
- MoneySuperMarket
- Which?
- Comparison websites won't all give you the same results, so make sure you use more than one site before making a decision. It is

also important to do some research into the type of product and features you need before making a purchase or changing supplier.

- Plan for times when there's no rent coming in

Don't assume that your property will always have tenants. There will almost certainly be 'voids' when the property is unoccupied or rent isn't paid and you'll need to have a financial 'cushion' to meet your mortgage payments. When you do have rent coming in, use some of it to top up your savings account. You might also need savings for major repair bills. For example, the boiler might break down, or there may be a blocked drain.

Stamp Duty Land Tax (SDLT)for buy to let properties is an extra 3% on top of the current SDLT rate bands.

What to do if you feel that you have been given wrong advice
The mortgage lending market is very complicated and many people have suffered at the hands of financial advisors and others who have given incorrect advice. Mortgage regulation has not been very tight. However, the basic framework is as follows:

- Sales of mortgage linked investments like endowments or pensions are regulated by the Financial Conduct Authority. Anyone selling investments must be qualified and registered and must be able to clearly demonstrate that the policy that they have recommended is suitable. All registered individuals and firms are inspected by regulators and can be fined or expelled from the industry if guilty of wrongly selling products. By contrast, information on mortgages is currently regulated by the industry only, voluntarily, under a code of mortgage practice sponsored by the Council of Mortgage Lenders. Although most of the big players are signed up to the code there are still some who are not. Check first before taking advice.

How to complain

- Complain first to the company that sold you the product, going through its internal complaints procedure.

- If you are unhappy with the firm's decision, approach the relevant complaints body. For mortgage advisors employed directly by lenders, or complaints about lenders generally, contact the Financial Ombudsman Service on 0300 123 9 123 or www.financial-ombudsman.org.uk

- For mortgage lenders which are not building societies or banks but which are signed up to the mortgage code, the Chartered Institute of Arbitrators 020 7421 7455 www.ciarb.org will assist.

- If your complaint is about a mortgage broker, contact the Chartered Institute of Arbitrators which may be able to help if the firm is registered under the code.

- Complaints about endowments, pensions and other investments is handled by the Financial Conduct Authority 0800 111 67 68 www.fca..org.uk and are dealt with by the Financial

Ombudsman Service. The most common complaint is to do with endowments. A lot of people bought products which they came to regret. They are a major source of profit to the provider-and all those in between-but the person left holding the problem is the consumer. If you believe that you have been given bad advice about anything to do with the insurance or investment side of a product then you should approach the Financial Services Authority. The Building Society Association or the British Bankers Association have free publications that should help you. In addition, the Consumers Association, "Which" runs regular articles on mortgages. Remember - always ask questions. Never rush into anything. Always take advice if you are uncertain. Banks and building societies themselves are usually a better source, a safer source than individual advisers.

Borrowing and the internet

Almost all lenders have their own sites and many operate internet only loans with keener rates than those available on the high street. But there are also growing numbers of mortgage broker sites, offering mortgage calculators so that you can work out how much you can afford to borrow and how much the true cost of your loan will be. A list of internet sites can be found in the useful addresses and websites section at the back of this book.

Chapter 5

Selling Your Home

_____

Estate agents

Ask for quotes from at least three agents before instructing one or more of them. The fee is normally based on the selling price of the house and is between 1 - 3 per cent of the final selling price. However, VAT (currently 20%) will be added on to this.

Online agents

Should I use an online estate agent to sell my home?

Using an online agent to sell your home can save you hundreds or thousands of pounds. But can you trust them to handle your most important financial transaction? Whether you're thinking of the main players such PurpleBricks, eMoov, Tepilo, HouseSimple or YOPA, you need to know what to watch for

Why should I use an online estate agent?

Without a doubt, the biggest advantage of online agents is the savings you can make. High street agents typically charge around 1.5% of the price achieved. Even with a commission of 1.5% this means you will pay £4,500 if you sell your home for £300,000. This seems extortionate compared to fees charged by online agents where packages range from about £200 to £1000.

Can I trust online estate agents?

There is no law stopping either you or me from setting up as an estate agent tomorrow – on the high street or online. So how do you ever know if they are legitimate?

All agents must be a member of one of three grievance bodies who can pursue your claims should things go wrong: the Property Ombudsman, the Ombudsman Services Property and as of 2014 the Property Redress Scheme. However, their powers are limited so don't make the mistake of taking it as a stamp of approval.

What do I need to watch for when using an online agent?

There are a couple of issues you need to be aware of when using an online agent:

- First, you often have to pay up-front. That means that if the agent fails to sell your property you have lost that money. You might think the deferred payment option that many online agents offer would be a way round that but beware: you will have to pay this usually at the 10 or 12 month point whether you have sold or not. And these pay later deals often involve you signing up to a credit or loan agreement with a third party organisation so the agent can ensure they get their money back.

- Second, check the fee advertised isn't conditional on you using the agent's in-house services, like their recommended mortgage broker or conveyancer. This shouldn't be allowed but does happen. It's important you're able to shop around for the best deal.

- Third, speak to the online agent and check their package includes everything you would expect. No one online agent is the same and they all offer different deals. You should also ask to see the contract if there is one to check tie-in period and other contract terms.

- Fourth, ask the online agent you're considering instructing how they vet potential buyers to minimise the risk of time wasters or a sale falling through due to lack of funds

How will people find my property?

Like high street estate agents, online agents use Zoopla, Rightmove and other property portals to market your property. So while people won't find your photo in a high street agents' window as they go for a stroll on a Sunday afternoon, serious buyers will regularly check the portals. You will want to look at the different agents' marketing packages. "For Sale" boards are also offered by online agents – but double check that they will erect the sign for you.

Will I need to arrange viewings?

Most online agents will arrange the viewings for you and keep you updated by phone or using a dedicated online site just for you- but they won't usually attend.

If you work full time an open day where all potential buyers view the property in one day might be a good option. Discuss this with your estate agent.

Will I need to conduct viewings?

In most cases, yes. The online agent will not attend the viewings. Some agents will offer to attend viewings and show prospective buyers around at an additional cost which can soon mount up.

Increasingly "hybrid agents" offer to conduct viewings as part of their standard package price.

What is a "Hybrid Agent"?

"Hybrid agents" like PurpleBricks are online agents that also offer services traditionally only delivered by high street agents. In particular they conduct viewings for you using a local property "expert". This makes their packages more expensive than other online agents. Before going with an hybrid agent that offers to conduct viewings, you should ask:

- are your local experts qualified estate agents?
- how big a local area do they cover? (you want reassurance

that the local expert isn't covering so large an area that they will struggle to attend your viewings)

- are there any additional costs when the local expert conducts viewings?

How will an online agent value my home?

As online agents operate from nationwide call centres they are likely to have limited local knowledge, so valuing your house is often done using online data. That's fine as a guide but you really need people with local knowledge to help you set the right asking price. Be warned that this can also be the case with "hybrid agents" that use local property "experts"; the scale of the geographical areas each local expert covers usually means they don't know the specifics of your local market.

This shortcoming is easily overcome by asking three local high street agents to value your home before deciding whether to opt to go on-line.

Will the online agent negotiate a final deal with my buyers?

Some online agents will take offers, discuss them with you and negotiate the price for you, while others will leave it up to you. Don't want to haggle? Then choose an online agent who will do it for you.

Will they really care about my sale if I pay up-front rather than on commission when a sale is achieved?

Arguably, online estate agents do not have the same commission based incentive as a high street agent to get you (and them) the highest price possible, whereas high street agents will apply their experience and skills to do so. Assuming your high street agent knows what they are doing, of course. Online agents would argue that if they didn't do all they could to help customers sell their homes and provide a great service, then they would be out of business.

Is an online agent right for me?

Yes, if:

- You have time and don't mind conducting the viewings – or are happy paying more for a hybrid agent
- You like to feel like you're in charge of the process of selling your home
- You think you are better placed to sell your home
- You don't want to pay thousands to an estate agent when it feels like Zoopla and Rightmove do most of the sales work
- You can find the online agent that provides the right package and services for you

DIY Selling

It is possible to sell a property without using either a traditional or online estate agent. The process may take a little longer, but if all goes well the savings can be considerable. Of course, the DIY route is likely to take a lot of time and effort as the seller will have to grapple with all manner of people traipsing through their home as well as riding the negotiation and post-sale roller coaster.

Despite being the cheapest option, DIY sellers will still need to spend some cash. Firstly, you'll need to buy a for-sale sign, which you can obtain from firms such as Cheapmove.co.uk and Homesonsale.co.uk, typically for around £10 to £35. Of course, a board will only attract passing traffic, so you'll need to advertise in local newspapers and online. Unfortunately, not all advertising channels are open to the DIY sellers. Major players Rightmove, Prime Location and Zoopla only deal with professional estate agents, not private property sellers.

Setting the price if selling yourself

You need to see how much similar properties are sold for in the area. If this proves difficult, get a professional valuation. See Yellow Pages under Surveyors or Valuers or contact the Royal Institution of Chartered Surveyors. A valuation report will only value and will not assess structural soundness. A survey is needed for that. Put together the sales particulars in the same way that an estate agent would. It is advisable to put a disclaimer on these details such as "these particulars are believed to be accurate and are set out as a general outline only for the guidance of interested buyers. They do not constitute, nor constitute parts of, an offer or contract.

Advertising your property independently

There are a number of ways you can advertise your property. Local papers will advertise for you and also there are free ad papers. In addition, there are a number of companies with a computerised sales network who will charge you a flat fee for advertising. Be accurate with the details - you may leave yourself open to damages through misrepresentation. If an offer is made to you then you should then hand matters over to your solicitor. As discussed, some sellers handle their own conveyancing lock stock and barrel. This includes the legal side. However, this book cannot advise you on legal conveyancing. That is a separate matter. Suffice to say that it follows a standard format. It is easier, in the light of the reduced prices available to appoint a solicitor to do this side for you.

Quick sale companies

What are quick house sale companies?

Quick house sale companies offer to sell your home fast. They do this by buying your house directly, or finding a third party buyer very quickly. They pay cash for your property and usually buy at a discount rate.

Pros and cons of using a quick house sale company

Pros

Quick house sale companies can provide a useful service for homeowners who need to unlock cash in a hurry. For example to:

- Avoid repossession, clear debts or sort out financial issues
- Dispose of inherited property
- Move for age or health related reasons
- Sell as a result of divorce or relationship breakdown
- Relocate due to a change of job or to emigrate
- Try a different route if unable to sell through a traditional estate agent – get around issues that have made a property hard to sell, for example with a short lease or if a property has a high risk of flooding

Cons

Beware of unscrupulous quick house sales companies. One homeowner agreed a price of £120,000, only to be told the offer had dropped to £80,000 just before the deal was signed. Some companies agree to buy a house, but then reduce the price at the very last minute

- Fee structures are not always made clear to the customer

- Some companies make false property valuations
- Some contracts tie customers in, preventing them from selling to anyone else who might come along with a better offer

Is using a quick house sale company right for you?

To answer this question, you need to think about why you're selling and what your priorities are. Before deciding to go ahead, make sure you've considered all the alternatives (see below).

Alternatives to a quick house sale

Use a traditional estate agent

Before deciding whether to go ahead with a quick sale company, ask some local estate agents what price would get you a quick sale. You might find that the amount you need to drop the price by is less than the typical 25% discount that a quick sale company would ask for.

Negotiate with your mortgage company

If the reason you're selling is that you're struggling to keep up with your mortgage payments, contact your lender to discuss your options. Mortgage companies have to consider a request to change the way you pay your mortgage. One of the things they might suggest is extending the term of your mortgage (the amount of time left to run on the mortgage) to reduce your monthly repayments.

Look at other ways of funding your long-term care

If the reason you're selling your home is to pay for your long-term care, make sure you've looked into all the alternatives and have spoken to an independent financial adviser who specialises in funding long-term care.

Checklist for going ahead with a quick house sale

If you decide you want to sell your property through a quick house sale company make sure you:

- Do your own valuation: make sure you get a valuation from three different estate agents so you can decide whether any offer made by a quick sale company is fair.
- Shop around: not all quick sale companies are the same. Make sure you look at what different ones can offer.
- Check the company's credentials: If the provider is a broker (someone who introduces you to a prospective buyer), check that they are registered with either The Property Ombudsman or Ombudsman Services: Property. If the provider says they have signed up to a code of practice, or they are regulated by an official body, check for yourself.
- Don't be shy: it's always worth negotiating the terms and/or the price.
- Get everything in writing: don't accept verbal assurances.
- Take your time: don't rush or be pressured into a decision.

- Get your own independent legal adviser: the company you're using can't force you to use the legal representative they recommend. See below for where to find a solicitor.

- Read the agreement carefully: don't sign an agreement unless you fully understand what you're agreeing to. Get your legal adviser to explain anything you're not clear about.

- Avoid long tie-ins: don't sign any agreement that ties you to the quick sale company for a long time. A typical estate agency contract lasts 8-12 weeks. A quick sale contract should be shorter than that.

- Be honest: giving incorrect information or leaving important things out might cause hold-ups further down the line and even mean a reduction in the price you're offered.

- Ask to see the survey: if the company you're using reduces the offer price, ask why. If the survey's findings are to blame, ask to see them. A fair-dealing business will not hide them from you.

- Don't commit too early in the process: don't sign on the dotted line until all the surveys and legal checks are done and you have a final offer in writing.

Finding a solicitor

- **England and Wales** – find a solicitor on the Law Society website

- **Scotland** – find a solicitor on the Law Society of Scotland website
- **Northern Ireland** – find a solicitor on the Law Society of Northern Ireland websiteopens in new window

Questions to ask your agent

At each stage of the process, make sure you have all the information you need and you understand everything. Here are some questions to ask the quick sale company:

- Who is valuing the property and how?
- Is the company buying your property themselves or is someone else buying it?
- What are the timescales for the sale? What are the different stages and when will each happen? What might cause timescales to slip?
- If they are buying it, how will they pay for it? If the company says it has funds available immediately, ask for proof. A genuine cash buyer will be able to provide it.
- If someone else is the buyer, who are they and what guarantees can they give in terms of how quickly the sale can happen and whether the buyer has funds available?
- What fees and charges will you have to pay (for example surveys and lawyers' fees)? What are the fees and charges if you don't complete the sale?

- What might cause the offer price to change and when would this happen? Is the offer conditional, for example is it 'subject to survey and contract' or anything else?

Got a problem with your quick house sale company?

If you're not satisfied with the service provided by a quick house sale company, tell them and give them a chance to investigate and resolve your complaint. If you're not happy with the way your complaint is dealt with, you can refer the matter to:

- The Property Ombudsman or Ombudsman Services: Property (but only if the company you've been using has been brokering your sale).
- Call the Citizens Advice consumer helpline on 0345 404 0506.

Selling at Auction

Advantages of auction

In chapter 3, we looked at buying properties at auction. here are a few tips for you when selling a property at auction. An auction is an efficient and cost effective way of selling property and if prepared properly with intensive marketing, advertising and mailing, will result in the greatest possible exposure of the lots offered. To maximize the effectiveness of the marketing, considerable thought must be given to the guide price, which needs to be tailored to generate competitive bidding in the auction room, thus ensuring that the best price is being achieved. Although some properties are more suitable for sale by private treaty, taking this route does present uncertainties over terms such as sale price and timing of exchange and completion.

Selling by auction however, offers a high degree of certainty that a sale will be achieved on a given day and, significantly, on the fall of the gavel an immediate binding contract is formed. As no further negotiation is permitted the entire sale process, from instruction to exchange of contracts can be, is achieved within as little as six to eight weeks. For vendors with a large number of properties to sell, auctions provide a highly efficient method of sale allowing for a total or phased disposal programme selling in individual lots thus maximising receipts. For those selling in a fiduciary capacity, there is the added advantage of the sale being entirely open and transparent. Most types of property are suitable for auction provided that a realistic reserve price is agreed.

Who sells at auction?

Auction is now regarded as the optimum method of sale for many sellers who range from private investors and property companies to banks, housing associations and local authorities.

When do you want to sell?

Decide when you want to sell your property and which auction you would like to put it in. Sale dates and venues can be found on auctioneers websites.

What information do auctioneers need?

In order to give you the best possible advice auctioneers will need the following details:

Address

Description

Photograph

Tenure and Tenancy (if applicable) details

Floor plan or site plan

Anything else you consider to be material

Once the auctioneers have received this information, they will provide an estimate of the likely sale price of your property at Auction. Together with a proposed reserve, they shall send you a copy of their standard agency contract setting out their terms and conditions. Once the maximum reserve price is agreed you will be asked to sign and return the standard agency contract to confirm your instructions, at which time the Entry Fee becomes payable.

Proof of identity

If an auctioneer has not sold for you before they will require proof of your identity and address before they can market your property.

How much does it cost? Auction Entry Fee

All auctioneers will charge a fee to enter a property into an auction. This fee is payable whether the property is sold or not. The fee is a contribution towards the cost of marketing and catalogue production. The fee will depend on how much space is taken in the catalogue for the property.

In the event of a sale, an auctioneer's commission is up to 2% of the sale price plus VAT for a sole agency or 2.5% plus VAT for a joint agency. A joint agency is usually advisable where the auctioneer feels it is necessary to include a local estate agent to handle local enquiries and conduct viewing. The auction house surveyors will confirm the auction entry fee and commission rate with you in writing before accepting your instructions.

Sales particulars

Once the auctioneer has been formally instructed, the property will be inspected by one of their surveyors, measurements taken where appropriate, and the property will be photographed. Draft sales particulars will then be forwarded to you and to your solicitors for approval and/or amendments.

Legal documents

At the same time your solicitors will be instructed to prepare a legal pack containing special conditions of sale, title documents, leases (where applicable), searches, planning documentation and office copy entries so that they are available to interested parties either by post or on line.

Guide price

The auction team will recommend a guide price which you will need to approve before marketing begins. It is important to set the guide price at a realistic level which is attractive to buyers. This will generate competitive bidding in the auction room and ensure that best value is achieved.

Marketing your property

Marketing will usually start approximately three to four weeks prior to the auction sale. Auction Houses produce thousands of catalogues for each auction. These are sent to prospective buyers such as private investors, property companies and developers.

E-marketing

Catalogues are available online and auctioneers send regular email alerts to the private investors who are registered on the site.

Advertising and PR

Good auctioneers will advertise in the key property publications and place advertisements in local newspapers. Auction houses also target individuals who have previously expressed an interest in similar properties, as well as adjacent occupiers, local agents, local developers, builders and property companies.

Viewings and Surveys

Potential purchasers may want to view your property during the marketing period and have a survey carried out. You should let the auctioneer know how you would prefer viewings to be arranged and we shall arrange access for buyers. In most cases, vacant properties are open at pre-arranged times for viewing. Details will be printed in the catalogue.

Legal documentation

In conjunction with your solicitors the auction house will supply copy documents to prospective purchaser's solicitors and will keep you constantly updated as to the levels of interest shown.

The reserve price

The auction House will agree a reserve price with you for your property a few days before the auction.

This is the level below which they will not be authorised to sell. It is important that this be set at a realistic level.

Auction day-The Fall of the Gavel

On the fall of the Auctioneer's gavel, a binding contract is effected. The successful bidder is required to provide the name, address and telephone number of the purchaser and the purchaser's solicitors. The successful bidder will also be asked to provide a deposit for 10% of the purchase price. Identification of the purchaser is always checked at this stage. Clearance of all deposit cheques is arranged immediately after the auction.

Exchange of Contracts

The Memorandum of Sale is made up in the room and given to the purchaser to sign. The exchange is overseen by the auction house's solicitor. They will forward the purchaser's signed Memorandum of Sale to your solicitor.

Completion will usually, take place 20 working days later. The deposit funds are then paid to you less fees.

What happens if the property does not sell on the day?

If your property fails to reach its reserve in the room, someone may still wish to buy it. You will need to decide whether to accept any offer and advise the auction house accordingly. The property may even be sold in the days or weeks after the sale as we continue to market the property.

Quick Results

The entire process, from instruction to exchange of contracts, can be achieved within as little as six to eight weeks.

Chapter 6

Conveyancing a Property

Conveyancing, or the practice of conveyancing, is about how to transfer the ownership of land and property from one person or organisation to another. Land and property can include freehold property, leasehold property (residential) or can include business leases. *Essentially, the process of conveyancing lays down clear procedures for the conveyancer and also sets out each party's position during the sale or acquisition.*

Before understanding the process of conveyancing, however, it is essential to understand something about the legal forms of ownership of property.

Legal ownership of property

There are two main forms of legal ownership of property in Great Britain. If you are about to embark on the sale or acquisition of a house or flat (or business) then you will be dealing in the main with either freehold or leasehold property.

It is very rare indeed to find other forms of ownership, although the government has introduced a form of ownership called 'common hold' that in essence creates the freehold ownership of flats, with common responsibility for communal areas.

Freehold property

In general, if you own the freehold of a house or a piece of land, then you will be the outright owner with no fixed period of time and no one else to answer to (with the exception of statutory authorities).

There may be registered restrictions on title, which will be discussed later. The property will probably be subject to a mortgage so the only other overriding interest will be that of the bank or the building society. The responsibility for repairs and maintenance and general upkeep will be the freeholders. The law can intervene if certain standards are not maintained.

The deed to your house will be known as the "freehold transfer document" which will contain any rights and obligations. Usually, the transfer document will list any "encumbrances" (restrictions) on the use of the land, such as rights of way of other parties, sales restrictions etc.

The deeds to your home are the most important documentation. As we will see later, without deeds and historical data, such as the root of title, it can be rather complicated selling property. This is why the system of land registration in use in this country has greatly simplified property transactions.

Leasehold property

If a person lives in a property owned by someone else and has an agreement for a period of time, usually a long period, over 21 years and up to 99 years or 125 years, in some cases 999 years, then they are a leaseholder.

The conveyancing of leasehold property is, potentially, far more problematic than freehold property, particularly when the flat is in a block with a number of units. The lease is a contract between landlord and tenant which lays down the rights and obligations of both parties and should be read thoroughly by both the leaseholder and, in particular, the conveyancer. Once signed then the purchaser is bound by all the clauses in the contract. It is worth taking a little time looking at the nature of a lease before discussing the rather more complex process of conveyancing. Again, it has to be stated that it is of the utmost importance that both the purchaser and the vendor understand the nature of a lease.

The lease-Preamble

The start of a lease is called the preamble. This defines the landlord and purchaser and also the nature of the property in question (the demise). It will also detail the remaining period of the lease.

Leaseholders covenants

Covenants are best understood as obligations and responsibilities. Leaseholder's covenants are therefore a list of things that leaseholders should do, such as pay their service charges and keep the interior of the dwelling in good repair and not to, for example, alter the structure. The landlord's covenants will set out the obligations of the landlord, which is usually to maintain the structure and exterior of the block, light common parts etc.

One unifying theme of all leasehold property is that, notwithstanding the landlord's responsibilities, it is the leaseholder who will pay for everything out of a service charge.

Leases will make detailed provisions for the setting, managing and charging of service charges, which should include a section on accounting. All landlords of leaseholders are accountable under the Landlord and Tenant Act 1985, as amended. These Acts will regulate the way a landlord treats a leaseholder in the charging and accounting of service charges.

In addition, the 1996 Housing Act, as amended by the 2002 Commonhold and Leasehold Reform Act has provided further legislation protecting leaseholders by introducing the right of leaseholders to go to Leasehold Valuation Tribunals if they are unhappy with levels and management of charges and also to carry out audits of charges. It is vital that, when buying a leasehold property that you read the lease. Leases tend to be different from each other and nothing can be assumed. When you buy a property, ensure that the person selling has paid all debts and has contributed to some form of "sinking fund" whereby provision has been built up for major repairs in the future. Make sure that you will not be landed with big bills after moving in and that, if you are, there is money to deal with them. After a lease has been signed then there is little or no recourse to recoup any money owed. These are all the finer points of leases and the conveyancer has to be very vigilant. In particular read the schedules to the lease as these sometimes contain rather more detail. One of the main differences between leasehold and freehold property is that the lease is a long tenancy agreement which contains provisions which give the landlord rather a lot of power to manage (or mismanage) and it is always a possibility that a leaseholder can be forced to give up his or her home in the event of non compliance with the terms of the lease. This is known as forfeiture.

Under legislation referred to earlier, a new 'no fault right to manage' has been introduced. This enables leaseholders who are unhappy with the management of their property, to take over the management with relative ease. The Act applies to most landlords, with the exception of Local Authorities. These powers go a long way to curb the excesses or inefficiencies of numerous landlords and provide more control and greater security for leaseholders.

Check points in a lease

There are key areas of a lease that should be checked when purchasing. Some have already been discussed.

- What is the term left on the lease?
- Is the preamble clear, i.e. is the area which details landlord, tenant and demised (sold) premises, clear?

115

- Is the lease assignable- i.e. can you pass on the lease without landlords permission or does it need surrendering at sale or a license to assign?

- What is the ground rent and how frequently will you pay it? As we have discussed, the problem of escalating ground rents has highlighted the fact that properties can become difficult to raise a mortgage on due to the future outgoings caused by dramatic increases. make sure that you understand the ground rent provisions.

- What is the level of service charge, if any, and how is it collected, apportioned, managed and accounted for?

- What are the general restrictions in the lease, can you have pets for example, can you park cars and do you have a designated space?

- What are the respective repairing obligations? As we have seen, the leaseholder will pay anyway but the landlord and leaseholder will hold respective responsibilities. This is an important point because occasionally, there is no stated responsibility for upkeep and the environment deteriorates as a consequence, diminishing the value of the property.

Two systems of conveyancing

After gaining an understanding of the nature of the interest in land that you are buying, it is absolutely essential to understand the two systems of conveyancing property in existence, as this will determine, not so much the procedure because the initial basic steps in conveyancing, such as carrying out searches, are common to both forms of land, registered and unregistered, but the way you (or your solicitor) go about the process and the final registration.

Registered and unregistered land

In England and Wales the method of conveyancing to be used in each particular transaction very much depends on whether the land is *registered* or *unregistered* land. If the title, or proof of ownership, of land and property has been registered under the Land Registration Acts 1925-86 then the Land Registry (see below) will be able to furnish the would-be conveyancer with such documentation as is required to establish ownership, third party rights etc. If the land has not been registered then proof of ownership of the land in question must be traced through the title deeds.

Registered land

As more and more conveyancing is falling within the remit of the Land Registry, because it is compulsory to register land throughout England and Wales, it is worth outlining this system briefly at this stage. The Land Registration Acts of 1925 established the Land Registry (HM Land Registry). The Land Registry is a department of the Civil Service, at its head is the Chief Land Registrar. All applications to the Land Registry must be made within the district in question. There is a specific terminology in use within conveyancing, particularly within the land registry:

a) *a piece of land*, or parcel of land is known as a *registered title*

b) the owner of land is referred to as the *registered proprietor*

c) a conveyance of registered land is called *a transfer*

d) a transaction involving registered land is known as *a dealing*

The main difference between the two types of conveyancing *registered* and *unregistered* concerns what is known *as proof of title*. In the case of land that is unregistered the owner will prove title by showing the would-be purchaser the documentary evidence which shows how he or she came to own the land and property.

In the case of registered land the owner has to show simply that he or she is registered at the Land Registry as the registered proprietor. Proof of registration is proof of ownership, which is unequivocal. In registered land the documents proving ownership are replaced by the fact of registration. Each separate title or ownership of land has a title number, which the Land Registry uses to trace ownership, or confirm ownership. The description of each title on the register is identified by the *title number,* described by reference to the filed plan (indicating limits and extent of ownership). With registered conveyancing the Land Registry keeps the register of title and file plan and title. The owner (proprietor) is issued with a Land Certificate. If the land in question is subject to a mortgage then the mortgagee is issued with a Land Certificate.

Production of the Land Certificate

With registered land, whenever there is a sale, or disposition, then the Land Certificate must be produced to the Land Registry in the appropriate district. If proved that a Certificate is lost or destroyed then a new one can be issued by the Land Registry.

Key steps in the process of conveyancing-Legal Work

Your solicitor will examine the draft contract and supporting documents and raise enquiries with the seller's solicitor. You will be expected to go through the forms the seller has completed and let the solicitor know if you have any queries or concerns. In particular you will want to double check the tenure of your new home: is it leasehold or freehold? If it's leasehold, don't rely on your solicitor to check for the length of the lease. Leases below 80 years are a problem, can be costly to extend and you need to have owned the property for 2 years before you are eligible to do so. Leases under 60 years are best avoided.

Property searches. There are things you may not know about the property just from viewing it with estate agents or even getting a survey. The conveyancer will do a set of legal searches to ensure there are no other factors you should be aware of. Some searches will be recommended by the solicitor for all purchases and others will be required by the mortgage lender to protect them from any liabilities that the property may have:

- Local authority searches: are there plans for a motorway in your new garden? How about radioactive gas? This costs between £70 and £400 depending on the Local Authority and usually takes 1-2 weeks, but can take up to 6 weeks
- Checking the 'title register' and 'title plan' at the Land Registry– these are the legal documents proving the seller's ownership. The title register check costs £3 and the title plan check costs £3. Both checks are legally required in order to sell
- Checking flood risk – this can also done at the Land Registry. If you are already getting an environmental search (see below), you might not buy this one separately as the search will contain much more thorough flood information and maps
- Water authority searches – find out how you get your water and if any public drains on the property might affect extensions or building works. The water authority search will cost between £50 and £75

- Chancel repair search – to ensure there are no potential leftover medieval liabilities on the property to help pay for church repairs. This is a necessity and costs £18. However, you may decide to take out Chancel repair insurance instead for £20 or so. The laws around Chancel repair changed in October 2013 so now the onus is on the Church to establish and lodge liability with the Land Registry

- Environmental Search – this report is used on the vast majority of transactions and is provided by either Landmark or Groundsure. Depending which product your solicitor usually uses, the report will give information about contaminated land at or around the property, landfill sites, former and current industry, detailed flooding predictions, radon gas hazard, ground stability issues, and some other related information. The cost should be around £50 to £60 including VAT

- Optional and location specific searches – sometimes extra searches are required or recommended depending on the location or type of property or due to particular concerns raised by the buyer.

- These could include:

o Tin Mining searches in Cornwall

o Mining searches in various parts of the UK and Cheshire Brine searches o   Additional Local Authority Questions such as Public Paths, Pipelines, Noise Abatement Zones, Common Land, etc.

Your mortgage

You will need to get your mortgage in place. This will include ensuring you have the financing available for a mortgage deposit. Your solicitor will receive a copy of the offer and go through the conditions. You will need to get a mortgage valuation. This is carried out on behalf of the mortgage company so they know that the property provides sufficient security for the loan. You normally have to pay for it, but a mortgage company might throw it in for free to attract business. You will want to have any other necessary surveys done. Whether you have a survey done and what sort of survey you choose will depend on your specific circumstances.

Before exchange of contracts can take place your lender will require you to get Buildings Insurance for your new home. You are responsible for the property as soon as contracts have been exchanged so it is in your interests to do so.

Signing Contracts

Since receiving the draft contract from the sellers solicitor, your solicitor will have been in correspondence with you about what is covered. Before signing the contract your solicitor will need to ensure:

- That all enquiries have been returned and are satisfactory

- That fixtures and fittings included in the purchase are what you expected

- A completion date has been agreed between the two parties, which is usually 1-4 weeks after exchange of contracts, though this can vary widely

- That you have made arrangements to transfer the deposit into your solicitors account so that it is cleared in time for an exchange. You may want to negotiate on the size of the deposit, which is normally 10% of the value of the property. However even if you agree to pay less than 10% you are still liable for 10% of the value of the property if you later pull out of the agreement. Therefore if you pay a 5% deposit and pull out of buying the property you will not only lose your deposit but also legally owe an additional 5% of the value of the property

Go to the property with the estate agent and the fixtures and fittings inventory list to ensure that everything you paid for is still there and the house has not been damaged in any way

Exchanging contracts

You and the seller will agree on a date and time to exchange contracts at any time on any given day. Your solicitor will exchange contracts for you. This is usually done by both solicitors/conveyancers reading out the contracts over the phone (which is recorded) to make sure the contracts are identical, and then immediately sending them to one another in the post. If you are in a chain your solicitor/conveyancer will do the same thing, but will only release it if the other people in the chain are all happy to go ahead. This means if one person pulls out or delays, then everyone in the chain gets held up.

Once you have exchanged contracts you will be in a legally binding contract to buy the property with a fixed date for moving. This means that:

- If you do not complete the purchase, you will lose your deposit and owe the seller more if the deposit was less than 10%

- the seller has to sell or you can sue them

- the seller can no longer accept another offer (you no longer need to worry about being gazumped)

Between exchange and completion

Your solicitor will lodge an interest in the property which will mean that the deeds to the property are frozen for 30 working days to allow you to pay the seller and lodge your application to the Land Registry to transfer the deeds into your name.

The seller will move out (although they may leave this to the day of completion)

You should get organised for your moving day. See chapter 7, Planning Moving Arrangements. It is also worth considering the best day to move house to save money and ease the stress of moving.

The solicitor will send you a statement showing the final figure to pay, which will need to be cleared into your solicitors bank account at least one day before completion.

On completion day

Completion is normally set around midday on the specified date although in practice takes place when the seller's solicitor confirms that they have received all the money that is due. Once this happens the seller should drop the keys at the estate agents for your collection. You can then move in.

After completion

Your solicitor will tie up some loose ends:

- Pay Stamp Duty Land Tax on your behalf.
- He/she will receive your legal documents about 20 days after completion after your solicitor has sent them to the Land Registry
- Send a copy of the title deeds to your mortgage lender, who will hold them until you pay your loan off

- Notify the freeholder if the property is leasehold
- Give you a bill for their payment

You will want to collect together all your paperwork from the purchase of your new home, including the estate agent's brochure, to file away and keep safe for when you move again.

Bankruptcy of the vendor

In the unfortunate event of the vendor going bankrupt in between exchange and completion, the normal principles of bankruptcy apply so that the trustee in bankruptcy steps in to the vendor's shoes. The purchaser can be compelled to complete the sale. The trustee in bankruptcy is obliged to complete the sale if the purchaser tenders the purchase money on the completion day.

Bankruptcy of the purchaser

When a purchaser is declared bankrupt in between sale and completion all of his or her property vests in the trustee in bankruptcy. In these circumstances, the vendor can keep any deposit due to him.

Death of Vendor or purchaser

The personal representatives of a deceased vendor can compel the purchaser to sell. The money is conveyed to those representatives who will hold the money in accordance with the terms of any will or in accordance with the rules relating to intestacy if there is no will.

The same position applies to the purchaser's representatives, who can be compelled by the vendor to complete the purchase and who can hold money on the purchaser's behalf.

Chapter 7

Planning Moving Arrangements

Whatever the state of the housing market, the process of moving is fraught. Research commissioned by EstatesDirect.com put buying or selling a property as one of the most stressful experiences in life, above divorce or being made redundant. At the end of this chapter, there are useful tips to make the process less stressful. One thing is for certain, giving yourself a window before completing a sale or purchase until you move on to your next property is very important, if it can be managed.

The process of moving home is closely linked with the completion of the purchase of another home. That is, assuming that you are moving to another bought property. Of course, you may be moving to a rented home. However you choose to time your move, there are certain core tasks, as follows:

- Finalise removal and storage arrangements
- Contact electricity/gas/phone/cable companies and any other relevant company to tell them your moving date
- Organise your funds so that you can transfer all remaining

money needed to complete the sale into your solicitors account for him/her to pay the sellers solicitor

One main question is: do you get a removal firm or do you do it yourself?

DIY moves

This is cheaper than hiring a removal company, especially if you have a few possessions or no big items of furniture. You will also need willing and able friends. However, do not take the decision to move yourself lightly. Think carefully about the amount of furniture that you have and the fact that your house may be a particularly difficult site to move from.

Using professionals

Professionals know what they are doing and can leave you to organise all the other aspects of moving whilst they do the donkey work. This may cost you more money. However, it may be well worth it. Use a firm which is a member of the British Association of Removers (www.bar.co.uk). Members of this body have to adhere to a code of professional practice, meet minimum standards and provide emergency service and finance guarantees.

Removers can offer various levels of packing services. The most expensive option is for the remover to pack everything. The second most expensive option is for them to pack the breakable things such as glass. The cheapest way is for the removers to provide crates and for you to do your own packing. If you are going for the professional option:

- Get two or three estimates. You can find the names of local firms through the British Association of Removers, through the yellow pages (www.yell.com) or through Thomson's Directories (www.thomweb.co.uk)
- There are a growing number of websites that include quotes from removal firms (see below)
- You should expect estimators to go through your whole property including gardens and loft
- Check whether your possessions will be covered by your household insurance policy and extend the cover if they are not.
- Don't wait to exchange contracts to organise removers.

The following Websites may be useful:

www.reallymoving.com
This site was launched in 1999 and is the leading provider of online removal services. Registering on the site will get you three quotes from removers. It also covers solicitors, surveyors and others involved in the buying and selling process.

Contacting utilities

A boring but essential task is to contact all of the companies that provide you with services to tell them that you have moved. This should be done after you exchange contracts, obtaining meter readings etc. Most utilities will ask you for confirmation of your new address and moving date in writing. If you cannot face this task then use the following website:

www.iammoving.com

This site was started in 1999 by a consortium of investors and industry figures. The claim is to be the UK's first free online change of address service. You register, enter your old and new address, supply account numbers and meter readings where relevant and iammoving will send the information to the appropriate companies. The process is quick and relatively uncomplicated.

A few useful tips on moving

Decluttering

If you are put in the position of having a few weeks before you can move into your next property, then get rid of as much of your surplus possessions as possible as this will reduce the cost of storage.

Don't move at the end of the week or month

Try to avoid the end of the month or Fridays as these are the busiest times to move home These are the busiest times for removal companies and it will cost you more.

Hire a skip

If you absolutely do not need something, such as items stored in a loft, then throw it away. A skip is more convenient than multiple trips to the tip.

Don't move all in one day

Don't, if possible try to move out and in within one day as this will send stress levels stratospheric.

Parking restrictions

If there are parking restrictions outside your new house then apply to the council in advance for a day pass.

Chapter 8

Buying and Selling in Scotland

Scotland has it own system of law, and buying and selling a house or flat is quite a different process from doing so in England, Wales or Northern Ireland. The system generally works more quickly and there is less risk of gazumping. In this chapter, I will outline first the process of selling a property in Scotland followed by the process of buying a property.

Looking for property

Solicitors, property centres and offices. These are the largest source of properties available in Scotland. Often found in town centres, the property centres provide information in a similar way to estate agents outside Scotland. Also, the main websites, Rightmove, Zoopla etc all apply in Scotland.

Newspapers.

Daily Scottish newspapers are a good source of property. Regional and local newspapers carry many details on a regular basis.

Estate agents. These offer the same service

Ownership of property in Scotland

Property in Scotland does not exist as freehold or leasehold, as in England. Instead a "feudal tenure" system exists. This means that, as in freehold, the owner has right to building and land. However, the original owner of the development still has some say over any alterations and use of the land.

These feuing conditions are permanent and should be checked before purchase is considered. A new owner (feuar) can negotiate to have conditions waived, but there may be a charge for this. Further details of the system can be obtained from the lands tribunal for Scotland or your solicitor.

House prices

Property in Scotland is normally sold as "offers over" (sometimes called the upset price) the price set is usually the minimum and may not be negotiated down. This method is used where the property is likely to prove popular and to get the best price. If a quick sale is required a property may be sold as "fixed price" the seller will take the first offer at that price. If there is more than one prospective purchaser the seller may opt to set a closing date for offers. The process is then like a blind bid, with none of the buyers knowing the price anyone else is bidding. Although the seller usually accepts the highest price, this is not always the case; other factors, such as date of entry, may be taken into consideration.

When Selling a Property-The Selling process

The Home Report

From 1 December 2008 most houses or flats which are marketed for sale in Scotland will require to have a Home Report and to make it available to potential buyers. There are some circumstances when you do not have to produce a Home Report, for example if you are going to sell your property to a private individual without putting the property on the market. The person who is marketing the property is responsible for producing the Home Report. The responsible person will be you, unless you have appointed an agent to sell the property and have transferred that responsibility to them. There are three parts to the report: a single survey of the property, an energy report and a property questionnaire. More information about the Home Report can be found on the Scottish Government website at www.gov.scot.

Energy Performance Certificates

You will have to provide an Energy Performance Certificate (EPC) to potential buyers free of charge. Since 9 January 2013, when you advertise a property for sale you must include EPC information in the advert. The Energy Performance Certificate must include details of any Green Deal plan as the buyer will have to take over any repayments for the Green Deal loan. If you are producing a Home Report the EPC will be included in the Report. Failure to provide an

EPC can result in a penalty charge by the local authority of £500. If you are not required to produce a Home Report you must obtain an EPC from an agency accredited to Scottish Building Standards which is part of the Scottish Government. Details of accredited agencies can be found on the Scottish Government website at www.gov.scot.

There is information about the Green Deal scheme on the GOV.UK website at www.gov.uk.

Finding a buyer-You want to find a buyer yourself

If you want to find a buyer yourself, you can advertise, set a price, and show people round. However, you will need a surveyor to carry out the single survey and energy report for the Home Report. A selling agent can provide essential advice before a property is up for sale about the price that may attract the greatest interest, any repairs or decorating that will make the sale more straightforward, and whether or not there are likely to be any problems. These could be, for example, unauthorised alterations, or any necessary repairs. It would be advisable for you to find a buyer yourself only if you are familiar with the property market or already know of at least one person who is interested in buying. Although you can choose whether or not to sell the house yourself, the legal side of selling a property must be dealt with by a solicitor. Even if you are going to sell the property yourself, you should talk to a solicitor first, to try to ensure that there are no unexpected legal technicalities at a later stage.

Using a 'quick house sale' company

There are a number of companies that offer 'quick house sales'. A quick house sale provider offers to buy a property or to find a third party to buy it quickly, and usually at a discount. We discussed quick sale companies earlier and they come loaded with problems.

If you are considering selling your home using one of these firms, you should be careful. Before it closed, the Office of Fair Trading (OFT) completed a study of companies that offer quick house sales. It warned people about the risks of using some companies. For example, a company may reduce the offer to buy your home at the last minute. Or you may not be clear about who is actually buying your home, or whether they have the necessary finances in place.

Using an estate agent/solicitor as a selling agent

When you want to sell your property, in almost all situations, it is advisable to use a solicitor or an estate agent to act as a selling agent and to find a buyer. It may be more expensive to have a selling agent but they will take responsibility for producing the Home Report, advertising, negotiating a price for the house, and if necessary showing potential buyers round.

There is a range of issues that you should consider in trying to decide whether to use a solicitor or an estate agent to organise the sale. These are:-

- what the fee is — if only a solicitor is used it will be useful to get quotations from several firms as there can be differences. If an estate agent is used for selling the house, a solicitor will also have to be used for the legal side of the transaction. This means that it will be necessary to get quotations from both types of firm, perhaps several of each, to get an estimate of the fee. Quotations should include all outlays as well as fees

- whether either specialises in the type of property being sold or has particular local knowledge

- whether the estate agent belongs to a professional association. An estate agent must belong to an approved redress scheme. All solicitors firms are members of the professional association called the Law Society of Scotland

- what is known locally about the firms

- whether the solicitor or estate agent has been recommended to you by someone whose judgement you can trust and who has employed them before

- an estate agent can work for you and the buyer which can create problems of a 'conflict of interest'. A solicitor can act for only one party at a time.

Estate agents' and solicitors' fees for selling

You should check what is included in the fees for selling or whether you have to pay extra for:-

- producing the Home Report
- a valuation before selling
- advertising costs
- a 'For Sale' board
- VAT
- providing a viewing service.

What type of agreement can you have with the selling agent

Many estate agents provide a contract which specifies what services they will provide and what your rights will be, for example, to terminate the agreement. If you have problems with the agreement you may need the help of an experienced adviser.

Complaining about an estate agent

All estate agents must belong to an approved redress scheme. There are two approved schemes, the Property Ombudsman and the Ombudsman Services: Property. If you have a complaint that has not been resolved satisfactorily by your estate agent you can complain to the redress scheme that your estate agent belongs to. Estate agents that refuse to join a scheme can be fined.

Choosing a solicitor or conveyancer

Most firms of solicitors offer both an estate agency service and a conveyancing service. This is the technical name for the legal work in buying and selling property. Although most firms can take on this work, some firms concentrate on this area of work and have substantial experience. You should ask for written quotations of the fees and outlays and it will be useful to have quotations from two or three firms. Even if an estate agent has recommended a solicitor to you, you should obtain a quote for services and meet her/him before agreeing to giving their firm the work.

What a solicitor or conveyancer does

A solicitor may be involved in both the selling and the conveyancing side of the transaction. The main tasks involved include:-

- discussing your needs and explaining the procedures and costs of house sale including the production of a Home report

- receiving and accepting any offers for the property in consultation with you

- getting formal consent to the sale if you are separated from someone with rights to occupy the property

- checking title deeds and preparing a deed confirming the change of ownership

- getting searches of the official records carried out to check that you do have the title to the property that is up or sale and it is not subject to any legal action that would call that title into question

- getting the money from the buyer and where necessary repaying the existing loan on the property
- checking that all documents are correctly completed, signed and recorded
- negotiating with the buyer's solicitor.

If there are problems with the work the solicitor has done there may be grounds to make a formal complaint. Anyone wanting to make a complaint should seek the help of an experienced adviser.

A list of independent qualified conveyancers can be obtained from:-

The Law Society of Scotland
Atria One
144 Morrison Street
Edinburgh
EH3 8EX
Tel: 0131 226 7411
Fax: 0131 225 2934
E-mail: lawscot@lawscot.org.uk
Website: www.lawscot.org.uk

Deciding on the price at which to sell

If you are using a selling agent you should discuss the price you want for the property with the estate agent or solicitor handling the sale. You may advertise the property at a price described as 'Offers over...' which often means that you want no less than that price but ideally more. A property can be advertised at a 'Fixed price' which means that the first offer of that amount should secure the sale although, in some circumstances, a seller may accept less than the fixed price. When the property is small, and attractive to first time buyers, it may be important to set a realistic price as they may only be able to borrow what a surveyor says the property is worth.

It is important to discuss the situation with the selling agent as there may be different tactics on price to consider because of the type of property for sale.

Receiving offers

Your solicitor or estate agent receives offers from the agents of prospective buyers. If an estate agent is selling the property, s/he will have to pass the best offer on to your solicitor. A variety of offers may be made depending on whether you were looking for a 'Fixed price' or an 'Offers over...' price. If two or more prospective buyers have shown sufficient interest in the property to have it surveyed then it is likely that a 'closing date' will be set for the interested parties to make an offer. On the 'closing date' you can then choose the offer you want. You do not have to choose the highest one. If only one person is interested in the property a price can usually be negotiated between the agents of the buyer and yourself. A buyer may also submit an offer 'subject to survey'. This means that s/he is interested in the property but wants a price negotiated for the property before having to pay for a survey.

Accepting offers

An offer for a house includes certain basic terms such as a price, a proposed date of entry, and a large number of technical clauses, for example, about liability for common repairs or alterations to the property that have been done without proper permission. You may be advised not to accept the highest offer because other terms in the offer are not suitable. A solicitor must be involved in the process of accepting an offer. Once an offer has been accepted there is usually a period of negotiation between the solicitors for the buyer and yourself about the terms of the offer. During this time the sale is not legally binding and either side can break the agreement.

Deciding who to sell to

Whether you have arranged to sell the house yourself or you have used an estate agent you may find that you receive more than one offer for the house. You can sell the house to whoever you want and do not have to sell to the buyer who offers the most money.

It could be unlawful for a seller to treat people unfairly by discriminating against them. For example, it is unlawful to refuse to sell a property, or to offer it on less favourable terms, just because the prospective buyer is of a particular religion or belief.

If you use an estate agent to sell your property, then it is unlawful to discriminate against someone because of their disability, gender reassignment, pregnancy and maternity, race, religion or belief, sex or sexual orientation. If you sell your home yourself, it is usually only unlawful to discriminate against someone because of their race.

Concluding the Missives

The sale of the property is not concluded until full agreement has been reached between your solicitor and the buyer's solicitor on the terms of the contract. This is achieved by a number of formal letters passing between the solicitors. This is technically known as 'concluding the missives'. Once this stage is concluded neither the buyer nor the seller can break the agreement without having to pay compensation to the other party.

Completion of the sale

The sale is completed on the 'date of entry' to the property when you must have left the property and handed over all keys to your solicitor. Your solicitor must deliver the keys to the buyer's solicitor along with a formal document called a 'Disposition'. This transfers ownership of the property. In turn the buyer's solicitor must deliver a cheque for the full amount of the agreed purchase price to your solicitor.

Discharging the loan

If you still have an outstanding loan on the property this must now be paid off. This will be dealt with by your solicitor, who will obtain a 'redemption statement' from the bank or building society and repay the loan from the proceeds of the sale of the property. The solicitor should transfer any profit from the sale promptly to you once the transaction is concluded (Law Society of Scotland Practice Rules 2011, Rule 6.11.1).

When Buying a Property-The buying process

The steps in the process of buying a property in Scotland are similar to those mentioned above, with a few important differences. There are six main steps.

1 – Get a mortgage 'in principle'

Before you can put in a bid on a property, you need a mortgage lender to confirm that it is prepared to lend you money. This is called a mortgage 'in principle'. Without this, your offer won't be taken seriously. Properties are marketed with either a fixed price or 'offers over', which is the lowest price the seller will accept. Check your mortgage and deposit will cover the value of the property you would like to buy. Be careful not to overstretch yourself. Remember there are many other expenses you will need to cover, including mortgage fees, legal fees and, on properties costing more than £145,000, Land and Buildings Transaction Tax. Once you have agreed a mortgage 'in principle' you might have to pay a booking fee or other fee to reserve it. Typical cost: £99-£250.

2 - Find a solicitor

You'll need a solicitor before you can make an offer on a property. Solicitors are responsible for putting in the offer, negotiating and checking the contract as well as organising the transfer of the Title and money. When you've found a property you want to buy, your solicitor will register a 'note of interest' with the seller's agent. This shows that you are interested in the property and want to be kept advised of developments such as the fixing of a closing date to submit offers.

Submitting searches

Your solicitor will undertake searches in the property and personal registers to ensure that there is nothing which might prevent the seller from being able to sell the property. The solicitor will also check with the local authority to see if there are any planning issues that might affect the value of your property and whether any roads next to the property have been adopted by the local authority.

Most solicitors request payment for their work after completion but you might have to pay a deposit, or pay for searches upfront.

If the sale doesn't go ahead, but you paid for the search upfront, then you'll have wasted your money, so it's worth carefully considering this in advance.

You can also instruct your solicitor to carry out the search once the offer has been accepted but this will need to be agreed with the seller as a condition of the sale going ahead.

As a result, the seller might be reluctant to agree to this as the findings might give you a reason to ask the seller to lower their price, or even back out from the sale altogether. Typical cost: £250-£300.

3 - Home Report and survey

Before marketing the property for sale, sellers have to arrange a Home Report to show to buyers interested in their property. This must include:

- **Energy Performance Certificate (EPC)** - this reveals how energy efficient the property is and where improvements could be made.
- **Survey** – an assessment by a qualified surveyor from the Royal Institution of Chartered Surveyors (RICS) pointing

out the condition of the property, where repairs are needed and a valuation of the property. A mortgage valuation might also be included. The level of information contained in the survey is broadly equal to the Homebuyers report mentioned below.

- **Property Questionnaire** – sellers have to provide an accurate account of the property including its Council Tax band, any Local Authority notices served on it, alterations made, parking, any history of flooding as well as factoring in arrangements covering any repair and maintenance.

When you receive the Home Report for the property you want to buy, make sure to read it carefully.

It will give you a good idea of the running costs of your new home. You can also use it to ask the seller about utility bills.

Your mortgage valuation report

Once you have a mortgage in principle, your lender will arrange for a mortgage valuation to make sure the property you're buying is worth the price you're paying. Your mortgage lender might rely on the mortgage valuation contained in the Home Report if it includes one or needs an independent one. Typical cost: £150-£1,500 depending on the value of your property. Some mortgage deals come with free valuations.

You will also need to decide if you wish to rely on the survey contained in the Home Report or obtain your own survey. The surveyor who prepared the survey contained in the Home Report has a statutory duty of care to the seller who instructed it and to you as the buyer.

Surveys

If you decide to get your own, there are three types of survey:

- **Home condition survey** – the cheapest and most basic survey. Suitable for new-build and conventional homes, but not useful for spotting any issues with the property.
- Typical cost: £250.
- **Homebuyer's report** – a more detailed survey looking thoroughly inside and outside a property. It also includes a valuation. Check whether you can get the valuation and homebuyer's report done at the same time to cut costs.
- Typical cost: £400+.
- **Building or structural survey** – the most comprehensive survey suitable for an older building or one of non-standard construction (for example, if it's made of timber or has a thatched roof).
- Typical cost: £600+.

4 – Making an offer

Once you have the survey results, and are happy with what it says, you need to decide how much you're going to offer. The amount you offer will depend on:

- Property prices in the area;
- How much you can afford;
- Any competing interest in the property; and
- Anything else you wish to be included in the offer such as fixtures and fittings.

Your solicitor will do this in in a formal letter.

If there are several competing bids, the seller's solicitor will open them at the same time on the closing date and ring your solicitor to tell you if you've been successful or not. You might wish to wait until your offer is accepted before having your own survey done, in which case you make your offer subject to survey.

If your offer is accepted

If your offer is accepted, the seller's solicitor issues a qualified acceptance, which means that the property will be yours if contract details can be worked out. The solicitor will also hand over information about the property such as the title deeds and planning papers. Go through everything you receive with your solicitor as they might raise queries about the paperwork. Neither you nor the seller is committed yet.

5 – Agreeing the contract

Once all the contract details have been agreed, the two solicitors exchange letters.

These letters are known as 'conclusion of missives'. Both parties are now legally committed to the sale.

After the conclusion of missives you might have to pay a holding deposit – typically £500-£1,000 – to secure the deal.

It is not all that common to be required to pay this holding deposit as there are usually penalty fees in the contract to deter either party from backing out at this stage.

Once you've agreed the contract, you need to shop around for buildings insurance.

Title burdens

Your solicitor will check the title deeds and discuss with you the 'title burdens' – conditions attached to owning the property ranging from where rubbish bins can be put to more serious restrictions on how the property can be used and altered.

The seller then signs the transfer of the title deeds, known as the 'disposition'.

Contact your lender

Next, you or your solicitor should contact your mortgage lender and let them know that the purchase is going ahead along with the proposed date of entry. This will allow your lender to issue their loan and security instructions to their nominated solicitor. In addition, this will also allow the lender to prepare the release of their loan monies to allow the sale to complete on the date of entry.

The arrangement fee

There is often a fee to set up the mortgage – usually referred to as an arrangement fee.

In many cases this can be added to your mortgage, but choosing this option means you'll pay interest on it for the length of the mortgage. As a result you'll pay more in the long run than if you paid for it upfront.

6 – Completion and final steps

After your offer has been accepted, the sale will be completed on the date of entry agreed with the seller.

The seller's solicitor will ask your lender for the remaining money owed (usually 90% if you had to pay a holding deposit) in preparation for the date of entry.

If you are a cash buyer you'll need to pay the rest of the purchase price via your solicitor.

Other fees you may need to pay now

Your lender might ask you for:

- A fee for transferring the money, typically £40-£50
- A fee of £100-300 for setting up, maintaining, and closing down your mortgage account.

The seller's solicitor will also prepare the Land Transaction Return for you to sign.

You'll need to pay your solicitor's bill at this stage, minus any deposit already paid. Typical cost: £400-£900 plus 20% VAT. If you haven't yet paid for searches , their cost will be included in the bill along with other fees paid on your behalf. They will also arrange for the signed title deeds to be registered with the Land Register. The cost starts at £60 and rises , depending on how much you've paid for the property.

Your solicitor will complete the transaction by paying the Lands and Buildings Transaction Tax (LBTT) due. This is a new tax introduced on the 1st April 2015 for homes costing more than £145,000 and must be paid within 30 days of completion. The new rates will only be payable on the proportion of the total value which falls within each band. In Scotland, buyers will pay:

- 2% for homes that cost between £145,000 and £250,000,

- 5% for homes that cost between £250,000.01 and £325,000,
- 10% for homes that cost between £325,000.01 and £750,000.
- 12% for homes that cost more than £750,000.01.

The rate is 12% for homes that cost more than £750,000.01.

Chapter 9

Buying and Selling Overseas

Thousands of Britons have purchased properties overseas. However, this can be problematic and certainly basic advice is needed relating to the particular country where you are buying. There are a few general tips when buying abroad:

- Buy through a qualified and licensed agent. In most countries including France, Spain, Portugal and the USA, agents legally have to be licensed and using an unlicensed agent means that there is no comeback if things go wrong.

- Do not sign anything until you are sure that you understand it. Note that estate agents in the above countries will tend to do more of the legal work than in Britain and hence charge more commission.

- Always hire a solicitor (English speaking if you are not fluent in the local language) to act for you. In some countries, the locals do not use solicitors but you should insist. The solicitor will check that the seller owns the property and that there are no debts attached to it and that planning regulations have been met.

Local searches are not as regulated as they are in the UK and it's often a case of making informal enquiries at the local town hall.

- Understand the role played by the state notary (notaire in France, notario in Spain) he or she is a state official, whose only role is to see that the sale is completed. He or she will not act for you or the seller.

There are a number of useful websites where more information can be gained:

www.french-property-news.com

This site is the online arm of the magazine French Property News. It claims to have the most comprehensive list of properties on the web and also has details of other organisations.

www.french-property.com

Similar to the above

For property in Spain, try www.spainpropertyportal.com which specialises in Spanish property sales.

For property in Eastern Europe you should go to www.eurobrix.com

Other useful websites:

For the USA-

www.primelocation.com

www.propertyshowrooms.com

www.escape2usa.co.uk

Property overseas generally

www.property-abroad.com

There are many other websites dealing with buying and selling property in most countries of the world. It goes without saying that you should learn as much about a country as possible and deal with professionals only before taking the plunge overseas.

Useful websites

The Buying Process-general

The Local Government Association

www.lga.gov.uk

Confederation of Scottish Local Authorities

www.cosla.gov.uk

Greater London Authority

www.london.gov.uk

The Environment Agency

www.environment-agency.gov.uk

www.homecheckuk.com

House Prices

Halifax www.halifax.co.uk

Nationwide www.nationwide.co.uk

Land Registry www.landreg.gov.uk

www.zoopla.co.uk

www.ourproperty.co.uk

Property Search Sites

www.hometrack.co.uk

www.rightmove.co.uk

www.zoopla.co.uk

www.findaproperty.com

www.primelocation.com

www.onthemarket.com

www.home.co.uk

findahood.com

propertynetwork.net

findproperly.co.uk

propertyauctionaction.co.uk

uniquepropertybulletin.co.uk

speedflatmating.co.uk (links those with rooms and those in need of a room)

The buying and selling process-law and taxation

The Law Society www.lawsoc.org.uk

The Council of Mortgage Lenders www.cml.org.uk

HM Customs and Revenue www.hmrc.gov

Scotland

Law Society of Scotland www.scotlaw.org.uk

Leasehold/freehold

Lease www.lease-advice.org

Association of Residential Managing Agents

www.arma.org.uk

Mortgage search sites/brokers

Money facts www.moneyfacts.co.uk

www.moneysupermarket.co.uk

www.moneynet.co.uk

New homes

NHBC www.nhbc.co.uk

Renting and Letting

Association of Residential Letting Agencies (ARLA)

ARLA Administration

Maple House

53-55 Woodside Road

Amersham

Bucks

HP6 6AA

Tel: 01923 896555

Website: www.arla.co.uk

Email: info@arla.co.uk

Auctions

www.propwatch.com

www.primelocation.com

www.bbc.co.uk/homes/property/buying_auction

www.propertyauctions.com

www.netguide.co.uk/Buying_A_House_At_Auction

propertyauctionaction.co.uk

Index

❖